Bless the Beasts

❧

Bless the Beasts

A SPIRITUALITY OF ANIMAL CARE

Jeffrey G. Sobosan

CROSSROAD • NEW YORK

1991

The Crossroad Publishing Company
370 Lexington Avenue, New York, NY 10017

Copyright © 1991 by Jeffrey G. Sobosan

Printed in the United States of America
Typesetting output: TEXSource, Houston

Library of Congress Cataloging-in-Publication Data

Sobosan, Jeffrey G., 1946–
    Bless the beasts : a spirituality of animal care / Jeffrey G.
Sobosan.
      p.   cm.
   ISBN 0-8245-1135-2 (pbk.)
    1. Animals—Religious aspects—Christianity. 2. Spirituality.
I. Title.
BT746.S63 1991
242—dc20   91-18909
                                           CIP

For Tom
whose friendship
beyond the words of gratitude
came undeserved
like the finding of a shark's tooth on an open beach
into the life of this quite ordinary man

BUT ASK THE BEASTS,

AND THEY WILL TEACH YOU;

THE BIRDS OF THE AIR,

AND THEY WILL INSTRUCT YOU;

THE FISH OF THE SEA,

AND THEY WILL DECLARE UNTO YOU.

Job 12:7–8

Contents

Contents

Preface

I know certain people, though only a handful, who have an abiding respect for all the forms animal life can take, from the caterpillar crossing the walk in front of them to family, friends, and colleagues. They do not always articulate this respect very well, frequently saying they simply have a feeling that this is the way they should behave. Yet the simplicity of their statement indicates a sensitive, intuitive awareness that non-human life matters; that it has value in and of itself, independent of the uses to which we put it, and therefore must be treated with diligent care and an honor that circumstances, such as human convenience or greed or gluttony, should never abrogate. There is generosity in this attitude, an abundance of gentle and responsive temperament that gives grace to human abilities even when many others deny this same attitude in their own behavior. I have striven greatly to make this generosity my own, though I am not too happy with my progress so far, and this book is one of the results of this striving.

I offer what follows as a "spirituality of animal care." It is right that I define what I mean by a spirituality, and in this task I would like to paraphrase a definition drawn from Hans Urs von Balthasar, simply because I know of no superior one. The great Swiss theologian says that a spirituality may be defined as that basic practical or existential attitude that is the consequence and expression of the way in which a person understands his or her religious — or more generally, ethically committed — existence; the way in which he or she acts habitually throughout life according to objective and ultimate insights and decisions. This is a heady description, but I think it captures exactly what a spirituality is and so gives definite shape to the meaning of a word frequently wrapped in ambiguity. Furthermore, it gives seriousness to the task of formulating a spirituality for oneself (or spiritualities, for the varying dimensions of one's existence) that indicates that this task is not to be identified, as it often is, with the performances of mere piety.

So much of the writing being done in contemporary spirituality falls into one of two categories. It is written for the specialist familiar with complicated subtleties of thought, technical vocabularies, major and minor historical movements. It is spirituality for the professional scholar and the extraordinarily diligent non-professional lay person. Or it is written at the level of extreme popularization, the way a dimestore novel might be, and requires little more than an ability to read simple sentences composed of words any seventh-grader would recognize. The difficulty with the first category of spirituality is precisely its elitist audience; it will appeal to only a few and appear unconcerned with the ordinary living of most men and women. The difficulty with the second category, on the other hand, is precisely its over-popularization; too often the reader comes away having learned nothing, not even freshly consoled or encouraged. In this book I want to tread a path between these two categories. I don't want the reader lost in a sea of technicalities presuming a specialist's education. But I also don't want the reader to finish these pages without them bringing something new to his or her way of thinking. My intention for the book, therefore, is to be more descriptive than analytical (though there is analysis); to employ commonplace, or not so commonplace, images and experiences more than the results of scholarly research. It has been written to create (perhaps only to resurrect) attitudes that bless and enliven the care of animals.

One final word to this Preface. There is no such thing as a completely open mind. By this I mean that no writer works his or her craft, no analyst offers observations without some dominant idea or set of ideas — what we might call a "rubric of understanding" — influencing the topics chosen and what the author says about them. In this sense all writing, every analysis involves an act of faith, the faith that the author's rubric of understanding is a good one, deserving attention and expression. In what follows it will soon become obvious that the dominant rubric of understanding I have employed in my remarks comes from my love of animals and my own particular perception of the message of Jesus. I say this, however, not as an apology, let alone an excuse. I say it only in recognition of the fact that a completely open mind is a fiction; that my mind, like all others, is shaped in its thinking by feelings and ideas I have judged worthy of devotion.

CHAPTER ONE

❧

The Song of Baby Turtles

❧

Some memories just don't leave us alone. They don't age gently into growing dimness, then forgetfulness. They stay alive, alert, and effective. Some of them give us peace, or a joy that leaps to smiles, even laughter when rehearsed. Others clog our feelings of freedom, reminders of possibilities we were too foolish or naive or plain stubborn to entertain. Others still are the salt in our tears, the banshees that rise unbidden to plague our minds with anger, bitterness, the hurts we have tried to kill with present goals and future hopes but that mercilessly stay alive. Memories are like that. They are the parents of what we think we are, what we think we can or should be. It is to one of these memories of my own that I wish to turn.

My childhood was a lovely one, from ages four to nine. My family lived by the edge of a woods on a large island in New

York, though now the woods are gone, the trees giving way to monuments of commerce, the streams and ponds to parking lots. I was an energetic child, bright in school, and beloved by my parents. And as it was the early 1950s, and since I was an American boy, I was enchanted like many others by that singular phenomenon of sport, the "well-mannered game" called baseball. At age six I was already on a Little League team and saw little else of use in life than time spent in competing with other teams. My parents smiled at this, my sister ridiculed it, and my older brother took a stance of knowing approval. All my friends were likewise on teams and our conversations concerned little else than the last game played or the one played next. We were all what Kierkegaard would call little aesthetes, not caring much beyond the near past, even less beyond the near future.

The field where we practiced was on the other side of the woods from our home. There were two ways to get there. One could walk around the woods, a journey of about two miles, but safe and satisfying to a mother's heart. The other was by a path through the woods, well-worn but without the comforting presence of passers-by and streetlights and sidewalks. Needless to say, it was the path I preferred, during all times and seasons. Of particular delight was a small stream that cut it twice on my way to the playing field. I always stopped to examine its tiny inhabitants, and in an act of communion with them — though at the time I scarcely thought of it as such — I would often drink the water in which they lived. Short of my parents' embrace, sitting by that stream was my favorite place to be in the world.

The dark, hateful memory now emerges. It was a warm day in July and I was walking through the woods on my way to a practice game at the playing field. I was about two hundred feet from the stream's first crossing of the path when I spied a team mate ahead. He had a baseball bat in his hands and, tossing what I took to be small stones in the air, was practicing his swing. I moved toward him briskly, shouting his name so I wouldn't take him by surprise. But as I approached I noticed something peculiar — the wood on his bat was discolored, an odd sight since I knew him to be meticulous about the cleanliness of his equipment. Since he had acknowledged my shouting only peremptorily and had begun almost frantically to continue his batting practice, I became uneasy. Something was wrong. His hurried movement spoke the desire to finish what he was doing before I got too close to the scene.

He failed. When I was thirty feet from him I realized it was not stones at all he was batting; when I was twenty feet I saw the results of his effort lying on the ground around him; when I was ten feet I knew with rising sickness what he was doing. My team mate had found a clutch of baby turtles, perhaps fifteen in all, and one by one he was throwing them into the air and hitting them on the way down with his bat. Most he had killed instantly; all that was left of them was bloodied white tissue clinging to broken shells. Others were still alive, squirming on the ground yet unable to move, hacked and battered and beaten until death was only minutes away. Across the stream I quickly noticed a larger adult turtle whom I thought — though I knew it extremely unlikely — might be the mother of these babies. She remained still, neck craning, and for all the world the moisture dappling her face looked like tears.

There is an expression, "to see red," when describing blind fury. I'm not sure for how many people it is more than just a turn of phrase. But in the few times I have experienced blind fury a featureless cloak does seem to descend before my eyes and I become nearly blind to my surroundings. I grabbed the bat from my team mate's hand — he had begun to move away from me — and with a screaming swing I hit him on his shoulder. I wanted to hit him on the head, but the cloak of my fury was not that thick; a small light of reasoning thought came through and I realized a blow to the head might kill him. But I wanted to hurt him, hurt him badly enough that he would never forget the savagery he had so easily unleashed on a clutch of baby turtles. I found out later that his shoulder had been fractured, but that he never told his parents the true cause. I never told mine either, and my team mate and I never spoke to each other again.

After he had left I bent down to see if any of the baby turtles still living had a chance for continued survival. None did, so I left them, never being able, as the saying goes, to put an animal "out of its misery." But before I did, two things happened. As I was leaning over to examine the still living I swear to this day I heard a sound coming from them. It was like a low pitched wail, without melody, a confused and rambling song, a dirge of disconcerting tunelessness weeping a final word on life. It unnerved me enormously and made me join the weeping. The second thing that happened was that I crossed the stream and picked up the older turtle. I took her home and kept care of her for five years, until I awoke one morning with a start, sure that something had gone very wrong while I slept, and she was dead.

∽

Some biologists tell us that below a certain level of neural development an organism does not feel pain. This may be so, but even an amoeba will respond erratically when a slight electric current is released into its surrounding environment. And who is to say definitely that this response is not one of pain? At any rate, there is no doubt that all the "higher" animals — reptiles, birds, mammals, primates — do experience pain; even baby turtles will writhe in unquestionable agony when slugged with a baseball bat. Medical researchers and veterinarians also assure us that such pet animals as cats and dogs are subject not just to physical pain but kinds of psychological pain as well. They experience moroseness when a favored owner is too long absent, loneliness when a companion of its own kind is no longer within reach, frustration when a desire is chronically unmet. There is an accompanying refusal to eat, exercise, respond to lures or commands; at an extreme the animal will even ignore the instinct to survive and slowly deteriorate until death intervenes.

How might we approach the above situation? First of all, and obviously, we can ignore it. We can judge it too insignificant to shape a forming influence on our behavior. People choosing this response typically fall into one of two categories. There are those who decide, with varying degrees of consciousness, that there are sufficient concerns centering on the fate of their own lives to prohibit concern for the lives of animals — taken to its limit, even other human lives. The problem engendered by this response is the severe stricture it places on the capacities of human care, the richness of affection it diminishes. A second category includes those who decide, again with varying degrees of consciousness, that there is enough human pain in the world to garner our attention, that sympathy for animal pain is a deflection from this, and that our responsibility is therefore to exhaust ourselves in caring for our own kind. The problem engendered by this response lies in the way it foreshortens our awareness of the sanctity of all life, not just human, its species egocentricity, and its refusal to acknowledge that before the whole world of life the proper response is not a selective care but an overreaching and active humility and reverence.

A second approach we have already touched on. We can adopt the tack that animals do not feel pain, or at least do not feel it the same way we do. We can dismiss the significance of this option immediately. There isn't a reputable research scientist who will support it (except perhaps for very simply organized life forms), nor would anyone else with a tidbit of sensitivity to his or her experiences of an animal's response to external stimuli. Shove a lit cigarette against a cat's nose, step on a dog's foot, yank out the tail feathers of a parakeet, or bludgeon baby turtles with a baseball bat, and you will note a behavior remarkably similar to your own in similar situations.

Human beings may be the only animals able to reflect consciously on their pain and seek a meaning for it. But they are not the only ones who experience pain, nor the only ones who learn from it. An ancient Taoist inquiry reads, "Can you speak of ice to dragonflies?" No, you cannot — at least if you're expecting comprehension of your words. But put a dragonfly on a block of ice and it will soon feel the freezing cold and take flight.

A third approach to the pain of animals is sympathy. The word comes from two Greek roots meaning "to suffer with," and it attempts to capture the delicacy of mind that permits us to share as our own the experiences of others. Usually its application is entrapped in intrahuman relationships, though there is no persuasive reason why this should be so. Sympathy can have a reach as wide as life itself, the feeling of communion and equality that allows a St. Francis to speak of wolves and sparrows as his brothers and sisters, or an Albert Schweitzer to speak against the vivisection of animals as if it were his own flesh being cut. Failing this sympathy we put a cloture on the richness of experience that all living things offer us. We also truncate the profound image of ourselves as the shepherds of creation, not its indifferent or tyrannizing overlords. The surest sign, then, that we have begun to appreciate the meaning of a spirituality of animal care is when we no longer ignore or demean but respect both the use and the beauty of the liveliness we find in the world.

The illustrious nineteenth century philosopher Arthur Schopenhauer said that he held three things against Christianity (though we may add that these same three could be held against other religions as well as many schools of philosophy). The first was its optimism, its silly optimism that refused adequate recognition of the pain of earthly existence in the hope for heavenly life, coupled with a corresponding refusal to do little or anything to ameliorate the causes of this pain. The second was its confusion between faith and doctrine, the inability to understand that the meaning of the purposes and objects of religious faith are forever developing and cannot be captured in dogmatic, immutable propositions. The third was its anthropocentric indifference to the suffering of animals, its preachings and writings that gave importance and reflective effort only to the causes and purposes of human pain. While in his first two criticisms Schopenhauer was in league with many other thinkers of his time, in the third he stood almost alone.

I have a pet cat who has lived with me for eight years. When I found him he was hiding at the base of a redwood tree on the campus where I teach. Mt. St. Helens had erupted the week before and there was volcanic ash everywhere. As I walked by the tree, whose branches reached the ground and whose trunk was a good fifteen feet from the tree's outer perimeter, I heard just the slightest crying, like the muffled sobs of an infant in the next room. I spread the branches, careful of the ash especially since I was wearing a new suit, and there, snuggled against the tree's base was the tiniest kitten I had ever seen. There was no delay, no debating within myself, no posing of pros and cons. I worked my way into that tree, cloaking myself with the damnable ash, picked the kitten up, and worked my way out. Passers-by looked at me as if I had been seized with dementia or were playing a bad joke on the elegance and good taste expected of a university's faculty. I was a mess.

When I got home I began examining the kitten, and with each passing moment my horror increased. His nostrils and ears were plugged solid with volcanic ash, so my guess was that he had been under the tree for two or three days. He was only three, maybe four weeks old — and later, when I tried to feed him, discovered that he had not yet been weaned. He also kept lapsing in and out of consciousness, unable to stand upright for more than a few seconds, with pupils that did not open and close appropriately with varying degrees of light. Worst of all, I discovered that he had been burned eight places on his body, including his genital area, with what I took to be a lit match or cigarette. I was convinced that all my impromptu medical care was only the final ritual before the death of that kitten. But I was wrong. In six weeks, with much attention and kindness of voice and touch, he had developed normal kitten behavior. Since then he has been a favored companion of mine, a lovely gift of the day when I heard his cries under a redwood tree.

Experiences like the above, from the slaughtering of baby turtles to the torturing of a baby kitten, have populated my life. They have made me enormously sympathetic to Schopenhauer's criticism regarding human indifference to the suffering of animals. Some people have considered me naive in this, and my own meditations have often highlighted what might seem an excessive response to the malice of which human beings are capable. The bald fact is that many people do very similar things to their own babies as is done to animals. The statistics on child abuse, from burning and stabbing to bludgeoning and smothering, are diabolic in their details and frequency. For what is so shocking about the brutalizing of a kitten when on Good Friday a young woman crucifies her two-year-old son against a garage wall? It is true that we can simply bow and accept such facts, acknowledging the evil in human behavior and hoping to get through life protected as much as possible from it. This is the way of the so-called hard realist. But I refuse to let thought stop at this point. There must be other options, other ways of looking at the life around us, attitudes that do not bow to brutality but seek to overcome it.

I've noted time and again in conversations with people that there frequently occurs a confusion between questions of ease and questions of possibility. It seems that at a certain point of difficulty tasks that are still possible are too readily described as impossible. Coupled with this I've also noted that we often fall prey to the seduction of giving up on a responsibility. This giving up — it's one of the easiest things in the world to do. It's almost as easy as denying the existence of God, since one can do that while sitting comfortably in an armchair sipping a martini. It is, I suspect, the marriage of this confusion between ease and possibility with our propensity to give up on tasks that largely explains why many of us do little to diminish the pain of living things, especially those not of our species. We must strive to break this marriage within us, because neither partner is worthy of our dignity. For while a distinguished theological tradition might speak of the weakening of the will as an unavoidable result of a Fall from God's favor, this weakening should not be understood as absolute. Our weakness can and must give way to strength, a strength that we will suggest in a later chapter is provided by receptivity to the grace in the world around us.

What is needed is an expansion of our ethical concerns and commitments. While we recognize, for example, that maliciously damaging another human being is wrong, we must extend this principle (even when at first we think it will be honored more in the breach than the keeping) to all living things. So too with such generally acknowledged norms as sheltering the homeless, feeding the hungry, caring for the sick. This task is not easy, but it is possible, and we must muffle in our spirits the sweet temptation to give it up. With the Buddhist saint we must strive toward that point where we can say, "All that is alive is a part of me, and I am nothing save for them." This is sanctity at a high pitch, beyond the concerns of formal religion, recognizing that non-human life includes not just the animals but God as well. For God too survives in our lives only when we protect and nourish our feelings for the divine.

In the face of very difficult tasks, when failure has greeted every effort at success, we are not always tempted to give up simply from indolence or exhaustion. Underlying these may also be the more profound experience of absurdity. We begin to ask the "Why?" of all our efforts, and can find no good answer. This experience is both debilitating and unbidden. It can come upon us suddenly, like a nightmare in the midst of pleasant dreams. The great master of the absurd, Albert Camus, to make this very same point once said that the feeling of absurdity can come upon us while standing on a street corner waiting for a bus. It suddenly blurs the meaning of our lives, begins to starve our spirits of worthy goals, and turns the sweet drama of our successes in life into a sour, embittered comedy. Whatever laughter used to scurry through our minds now turns into futile curses, or sighs.

When we look at the death all around us, the extermination of living things brought about in several ways, the encouragement to reverence and care for Earth's creatures may begin to take on the flavor of the absurd. In the eighteenth and nineteenth centuries, for example, the discovery in the fossil record of the extinction of whole species of plants and animals sent shivers of absurdity through even the best educated, most "objective" minds. The query it raised was not only a scientific one (Why had these species disappeared? Why had they existed in the first place?) but also a religious one (Why had a providential, benevolent God permitted these extinctions?). It was a time, after all, unpleasantly remembered by some scientists today, when science was still seen by many as the partner of theology, demonstrating through the intricate design of the world the presence of a divine hand. There is evidence that even the magnificent Isaac Newton, whose eminence in theoretical science is perhaps matched only by that of Albert Einstein (himself a thoroughly religious man), considered the piety born from his theology the motive and justification of his contributions to human knowledge.

The extinction of species still exercises the concern of some scientists, and to a lesser extent of some theologians as well. The history of this concern during the last two and a half centuries is an extraordinarily complex one, and I've no intention of addressing it here. For the interested reader, however, I could recommend the many luminous works of Loren Eiseley; less enthusiastically, the works of Stanley Jaki. The only point I wish to make now is that what this fact of species extinction required was a conversion in ways of thinking. Presumably legitimate scientific theories (that the existence of species was stable; that if we could find no living examples of some species, we hadn't scoured the Earth minutely enough) and theological ones (that God's benevolence would not permit the wholesale destruction of species) had to be reworked. I would remark, however, that in this process very few were touched by the magnitude of the death involved, the scourging and obliteration from existence (by the laws of Nature, or the will of God) of so many animals, some of them human prototypes. For many scientists, especially in this century, the fact of species extinction was only an intellectual problem, a puzzle to be worried through like one of Zeno's paradoxes.

Reworking cherished ideas is a painful procedure. But if old ideas are no longer persuasive, and if we wish to avoid the pit of absurdity, this reworking is precisely what is required. True, we can opt for the absurdity of our efforts, give them up and sink into sybaritism or a killing despair. But there is also the possibility, though it promises no ease, of a metamorphosis of thought, developing a different way of thinking that holds out a challenge to absurdity, that can loosen its choking tentacles wrapping our minds and give us new hope. Therefore, the knowledge that animals, human and non-human animals, die brutally and without apparent sense, on only one option issues in feelings of futility when thinking or planning action about this fact. On another option it becomes a catalyst for reformation in how we think, and as a result of this, in what we do. The key ingredient here, touched on above, is the experience of conversion.

The word "conversion" comes from two Latin roots: the prefix *con-*, which intensifies the meaning of the word following it, and the verb *vertere*, which means to turn. Conversion, then, means to turn, but because of the prefix it does not mean to turn just slightly but rather to turn completely around, to go in the opposite direction from which you were heading. Little word studies like this can tell us much about ourselves because they tell us about the language we use. From a term that at first was likely used to describe variations of movement, it came to have a larger compass when it also began to describe variations of thought. We know as well that a slight change in physical direction (say, when walking) takes much less energy and balance than when turning around. So again, the same can be said in changes in our patterns of thinking. To convert to a new way of thinking takes far more effort than merely refining or elaborating old ways.

I've already mentioned the conversion I have in mind. It is a conversion to sympathy, the active care and reverence for animal life. And I've also noted that the word "sympathy" comes from a Greek verb meaning "to suffer with," so that the reverence and care we exhibit are born from an intimacy, a type of identity with animal life that permits us to appreciate not just the bare life itself but also our responsibility toward it. Sympathy, I am now saying, is the twin of humility, the awareness that there are values more important than the dilettantism of satisfying superficial desires. It is humility that allows us both to laugh ("humility" derives from the same root as "humor") at the foolishness of so much that we do as well as cry when this foolishness turns brutal and makes us pain-givers to other life in the world. Without sympathy all that matters to us is ourselves, and this is a dead-end to any rich or vital meaning we wish our lives to possess. Detailing specific expressions of this sympathy is one of the major purposes of this book.

∽

About a mile from where I grew up on Long Island there lived an old man — old, at any rate, to a boy just celebrating his eighth birthday. He lived on what I guess to be about two acres of land and there kept a small menagerie of animals: chickens, a few ducks and sheep, and rabbits. He was a gruff man, though not mean-spirited or unkind, and I had a standing invitation to visit him and the animals whenever I pleased. My parents weren't particularly happy about this, though if I persisted they usually permitted a short stay with him. He was a drinker, three times divorced, and made a small salary when the mood struck by doing handiwork for others. There was a certain aura about him, a toughness of mind and mettle, a disregard for what he called the "'pinions" of others that greatly impressed (I can tell you truly) an eight-year-old boy. It wasn't that he ever provided an example for what I wished to become; it was that he was so *different* from everyone else I knew.

One day I discovered that doing handiwork for others was not the only source of his income. It was a clear, warm Saturday morning, the kind of day that stirs roaming thoughts in little boys. I decided to pay the old man a visit. When I arrived there was no response at the front door, so I made my way toward the back of the house. Even if he wasn't in, at least I could still visit the animals. But I became uneasy as I approached the backyard; there was a choking sound growing in intensity that set my skin with a slight tremble. As I turned the corner of the house I saw the source of the sound, grew faint, vomited, and slipped to a sitting position on the ground. In one of the pens nearby there was a rabbit with its throat half slit bleeding to death in a writhing agony.

As I said, the old man was not unkind. He spotted me at once, knew the source of my distress, picked up the rabbit, and hiding his deed from my sight killed it quickly. Then he walked over to me, filled with upset in his eyes, and sat down. He said that his knife was dull and did not cut cleanly enough through the rabbit's skin; that he had done a wicked thing letting the poor animal simply suffer and squirm until it bled to death. He was especially adamant that I not believe he did such things ordinarily (so much for his disregard for the opinions of others, or at least for my opinion). When I began to calm down he asked if I wished a glass of water. I said yes, and he disappeared into the house. While he was gone I stared at the bloodied corpse of the little animal and for the first time in my life I felt contempt (not the anger or puzzlement or frustration I had already known) for human behavior. The old man, despite his distress and the desire that I not think ill of him, disgusted me.

When he returned he began explaining why he slaughtered the rabbits. I suppose I could have accepted the idea that he used them as food, or sold them as such to others. But that was not the reason; he said he didn't care for the taste of rabbit and wasn't interested in the work of curing or smoking or freezing the meat, then wrapping and delivering it to buyers. No — the reason he slaughtered the rabbits was to skin them and prepare the furred pelt for use as table placemats. He would then send them to a distributing company and in return would receive, as he put it, a "handsome" payment. The thought entered and then stuck in my mind like tar on your best shoes that these little animals were being killed for no other reason than to satisfy the barbarity of people who wanted animal hides to decorate their tables. At that point I left the old man, pleading residual queasiness in my stomach, and vowed to myself that I would never visit him again. It was a vow I never broke, though on three occasions, when he was away from home, I released all his animals into the open woods.

Whenever I see a woman, or for that matter a man, walk by in an animal skin coat, I get angry. For I know that many thousands of animals are bred and nurtured solely for the sake of their pelts. They are not food sources — minks and foxes and leopards — but exist solely for the day when their skin is taken from them. This makes me angry not only because we have developed sufficient technology to make our clothes without killing life (cotton, wool, synthetic fibers) but because it offends the sympathy I mentioned above. And the oddest thing is that if people who purchased such items gave a moment's serious thought to how the furs were secured, many would be as repulsed as I — not simply from realizing the extent of the animal death involved but from the needless desire for mere luxury that causes this death. The indifference of others who refuse such reflection or blithely dismiss the thoughts it creates is symptomatic of a lack of sympathy that likely exhibits itself in other areas of their lives. There are people like this, trapped on one side of the triviality that, along with discord, Jesus condemned as a fundamental source of evil, a refusal to acknowledge the seriousness of what one is doing (the other side of this trap, which we will encounter later on, is giving an importance to something that it simply does not deserve).

But there is more. I have seen women carrying handbags made from the skins of baby alligators, sometimes with the head still attached. I was in a home once where an ashtray was made from the carved out foot of a baby elephant. I was even at a worship service where the priest proudly displayed at the foot of the altar a rug made from the skins of five monkeys. I have witnessed the barbarous vulgarity of the British when they take delight in their foxhunts. I have read accounts of the training of bull terriers to kill each other in dogfights, their blood lust encouraged by placing baby kittens in their training pens. I have watched young men at the seacoast shooting gulls as they flew by, a competition whose winner was the one who shot the most heads off without marking the rest of the body. I saw a boy who used baby turtles for batting practice. The macabre list could go on almost endlessly. And when I think at any length of such human obscenities, happening day after day, the anger in my mind has a way of changing into melancholy, the feeling of absurdity mentioned before.

I once came across an injured sparrow hobbling on the ground; its leg was clearly broken. Being a bit self-taught in veterinary medicine, I reset the bone, bandaged the leg, and then, despite chirping protests, began a regime of force feeding. In four or five weeks' time I took the bandage off and set the sparrow free. It flew in front of the rising sun and I will keep forever the sight of the dappling effect of the light on its body. It wasn't much that I did, a small effort for a small animal. But what matters is that it was a contribution, a giving of my care, of myself, to the furtherance of life. I remember thinking at the time that there wasn't anything of greater importance than this. The same thought is still with me, so that every effort I make at furthering life, protecting its many forms from avoidable pain and unnecessary death, is a consolation to me. It issues in a feeling of joyful usefulness, the conviction that as long as my life is used to assist other lives, my life has purpose and draws pleasure from a world often bereft of it.

It is this sense of contributing to the care of living things that I think is our access out of feelings of absurdity. If an individual can give back health to a sparrow, see it flying in the morning light, this can help overcome the sight of a seagull lying on a beach with its head blown off. This does not obscure the obscenity of the gull's death or the mindless savagery of those who caused it, but it can create the sense that an evil deed has been recompensed, if only in part, by a good one. And in affirming this we have affirmed our efforts, putting purpose where hopelessness once lay in our minds. But we have affirmed something else as well. For if religions are right in seeing the face of demons on the senseless deaths we humans bring about, then in touching the face of a sparrow we have healed perhaps we have also touched the face of God.

CHAPTER TWO

∾

Words That Create

∾

To give rhyme and reason to our experiences we became mythmakers in ancient time, and to this day we still are. A myth is a conceptual framework within which our experiences, now tied together and related to each other, begin to make sense. It makes no difference whether or not the myths are literally true; that is not their point — which is, rather, to enlighten the mind with insight or sympathy or hope for what we find happening in the world around us. When a myth is successful, that is, when its explanatory power is great, it tends to endure, sometimes for generations. So it is with all the great myths of love and friendship, animosity, heroic deeds, and restored life that still grace our finest literature. So it is, too, with the great myths of creation.

These myths are typically designed to address two fundamental inquiries (Why is there something rather than nothing?

Why are things the way they are?), and can conveniently be placed in one of two categories, both of which emphasize the activity of gods and goddesses: there is something rather than nothing because deities acted; things are the way they are because the deities acted in a certain way. The first category is that of deicide, the second is that of sexual love, commonly but not always within a marriage. We may note that an outstanding exception to these two categories are the creation stories in the book of Genesis, where the world is brought about simply by God speaking a creative word. The reason for this may be the incipient monotheism emerging in Hebrew thought (there are no other gods and goddesses to kill or marry) or it may be the result of mere polemic (Yahweh is so much greater than your gods and goddesses that he need only speak and things come to be). This second motive is still respected in the profound appreciation both Judaism and Christianity have for the power of the spoken word, no matter who is doing the speaking.

In the first category creation occurs through an act of violence. A good deity is pitted against an evil one, there is a battle, usually of cosmic proportions, the good deity wins, and in an act of revenge dismembers the body of his enemy, from whose parts come the various components of creation. In one account, for example, the evil deity, a goddess, takes the form of a giant serpent. When dismembered her eyes are tossed into the sky and become the sun and moon, her rippled skin is stretched to become the heights and depths of the land, her body fluids become the waters of the Earth, and so on. Most importantly, it is from her liver, supple and responsive to a shaping hand, that human beings are formed. What is intriguing about myths in this category is the implied judgment that since creation has its source in an act of violence and created things in the portions of an evil deity, then what is created, including human beings, must by nature be evil.

In the second category creation occurs through an act of love. A god and goddess join, and from this union children are born, spirit-beings taking the forms we see in the world. This is why a river is never just a river, a cat never just a cat, a tree never just a tree but divinized entities worthy of reverence and communication in rituals. And it is the same with human beings. In each of us, too, there is something of the divine, a spirit or "spark" of deity that makes us more than merely breathing flesh. Like myths in the first category, what is intriguing about those in this second category is the implied judgment that since creation has its source in an act of love and created things a sharing of parental divinity, then what is created, including human beings, must by nature be good. A similar conclusion also occurs in the first chapter of Genesis, where at the end of the days of creation we find the judgment, "And God saw everything that he had made, and behold, it was very good."

I do not want to argue here the merits of these two respective views of the nature of creation, whether it is good or evil. I will simply say that I side with the second, represented among other traditions by Judeo-Christianity, convinced that all creation is good, but that for a variety of factors this goodness can often be warped into evil. The winter mountain is good, though it may destroy by avalanche. The rains of early spring are good, though their waters can bring drowning floods; so too is the summer sun, though it may cause desiccation. The virus is good, but it can infect, and the caress of gentle winds can turn fierce and malignant. And human beings? We too are good, though the beauty of our behavior can sour into killing hatreds and crushing indifference. It is a question of what we can *expect* from creation. We can expect the good, though with the clear-eyed awareness that this expectation is not an inevitability. Everything is created good, but nothing is fated to be good.

The idea that in some privileged way divinity resides in all creation extends, of course, to the animals. But if we want to follow the implications of our second category of creation myths, then we do not want to say that animals (or the rest of creation) are gods and goddesses so much as that they are God's children. This distinction has not always been made. There are many illustrations where the animals themselves were worshipped as deities, if not in formal theological theory, certainly — as is often the case with religions — in the practiced theology of everyday piety. And perhaps nowhere is this more exquisitely described than in ancient Egyptian literature and art. There is the lovely Bast, the cat goddess of the netherworld, and her colleague Anubis, the jackal god. There is the vulture and the cobra, the deities that protect the destinies of upper and lower Egypt, represented on the double crown of the pharaohs. And there is Troth, the goddess of wisdom whose familiar is the calf, the very same calf whose image the Israelites made in the wilderness and for their efforts merited Yahweh's wrath.

I have nothing against the polytheism implied in the above description, neither aesthetically nor ethically. But I am also a child of Judeo-Christian history, the long and tireless effort to blot out polytheism from human minds and replace it with reverence for just one God. Oddly enough, though, the Christian cult of the saints, in my judgment a pragmatic if not theoretical polytheism, has enjoyed a robust life, with various saints, like the various deities in a polytheism, having more importance or influence than others. As with Egypt and its worshipped animals, so the literature and art surrounding this cult gives great beauty, pleasure, and consolation to religious sentiments. It offers a familiarity with holiness, an identifiable locus for the sacred that the worship of one God often lacks. So we read of peoples, in our culture commonly dismissed as "primitive," reluctant to cause the death of animals. In fact, in some instances when an animal's body is needed as a food source, the execution is preceded by an elaborate ritual of apology. It is not that such people believe the resident deity is killed with the killing of the animal but rather that the deity's home is being desecrated, bloodied then cooked for human need. I can tell you that in most countries of the world not even a remote remnant of this sensitivity exists to-day. Visit a slaughterhouse and you will witness animals, babies and adults, electrocuted with stun guns, striking three, four, five times until they are dead, without the slightest thought of the sacred life at home in them. This is an example of the advance on "primitive" cultures in which so many take such pride. But before the gaze of history as the tale of ethical progress, this pride is not only misplaced but a pernicious form of self-deceit.

Ancient ways are sometimes the best; not every change speaks of an advance. In a culture that still glorifies war, where armaments for human destruction are Satanic in proportion, and, despite the rhetoric of politicians, malevolent, not peaceful, in purpose, care for the animal life around us will likely be abbreviated. In a culture where species dominance is the order of the day, the Genesis permit to subdue the Earth and its creatures can be distorted into a blessing on human aggression and a refusal to apply benevolent standards of behavior toward non-human life. In a culture where avarice, luxury, and the spirit of accumulation are no longer understood as vices, the utilization of animals, or parts of animal bodies, to satisfy these desires will go largely uncontested. We could draw countless examples of the human brutalization of the Earth and its creatures. This brutalization is not just a problem of the perversity of specific individuals; it is, in my judgment, a massive cultural problem as well.

It is because of this cultural problem that, as confessed above, I am opposed neither aesthetically (because of the beautiful art and literature it can produce) nor ethically (because of the gracious behavior it can produce) to the spirituality underlying a polytheism that invests in all living things the spirit of divinity. What this means is that I am opposed to any spirituality that seeks to limit this presence to human beings, the type that unfortunately has prevailed throughout much of our history, at least in Judeo-Christian cultures. We must learn to make our minds more expansive, inclusive, more willing to embrace all living things so that the conceit that we alone are uniquely blessed by deity's presence will give way to the profounder thought that all creation, not just the human bits and pieces of it, enjoys a divine parentage. This establishes the parameters of an enormous effort we must engage in education, from pulpits and classrooms to dining tables and peaceful walks in the open air.

ॐ

I know an old woman who, like others, has become a bit foolish and silly and naive with the claims of age. She visited once while I was caring for an abandoned dog, an Australian ridgeback, for whom she took an instant liking. She cooed and caressed the animal so much that when she asked if she could take her home as a pet, I couldn't refuse. The old woman wasn't really a friend of mine, just an acquaintance, so a number of weeks went by before I communicated again with her. It was a phone call, and when I asked how the dog was, a long silence greeted me. I repeated the question, this time with some urgency in my voice, and waited until she replied. I refused to allow her silence to kill the question. She told me that the dog was dead, that she had died the week after coming home with her. The answer upset me greatly, as I too had liked the dog enormously. I asked how she had died.

The old woman began by relating how the dog had spent the first evening at home straddled between the couch and her lap, from seven in the evening until two in the morning. This was followed by a rendition of other bonding activities over several days that made the dog, as she put it, "like a child of mine." But then toward the end of the first week the old woman had to leave the house to run an errand. When she returned she found that the dog had chewed the corner of one of her throw pillows. A couple of days later, again being gone from the house a short while, she returned to find a small portion of her draperies chewed. I noted during her story that her voice had begun to quaver. What she was saying was clearly disturbing her. But then her tale turned quite bizarre. She voiced a conviction that she and the dog shared a closeness with each other, a type of love that others would not understand. Yet she also had her home, with all its fine, even valuable furnishings that she also loved. This second concern did not surprise me, since I knew her to be quite venal and overly involved with her material possessions. How could she keep the dog yet safeguard her furnishings? She decided she could not do both. So one night, convinced of her bond with the animal, that the dog would be miserable living with anyone else, she leashed her outside, went to the bedroom to fetch what she called her "security" revolver, and shot the animal twice in the head. By this point in the story the old woman was crying, and I slowly, gently hung up the phone, saying nothing further to her. The whole story seemed like something Sartre might have written a play about, or Hannah Arendt might have used as an illustration of the banality of evil, or Jesus of the wickedness we do when we think we are doing the good.

"Like a child of mine": these were the old woman's words. Yet clearly the animal was not like her child but more like one of her material possessions, something easily removed when no longer giving complete satisfaction. Contrary to her words she no more loved the dog than a spiritually sound person could love a throw pillow or a drapery. Earlier I spoke of the sanctity of animal life, its capacity to provide a home for divine presence. The old woman's words, "like a child of mine," now lead me to a few thoughts on anthropomorphism, describing animals not in terms of divinity but in terms of humanity. I find myself so frequently thinking of animals in anthropomorphic terms that, if I share this habit with you, I will feel myself much rewarded by your companionship. For sharing ideas, we know, can sometimes be an even more powerful bonding agent between people than sharing such things as parents, meals, money, flesh, and success.

"Anthropomorphism" has become a somewhat pejorative word. To many it means either denigrating descriptions of God to the limits of human capacities, or elevating descriptions of animals to capacities beyond their ken. It is considered archaic, even ill-mannered to speak of God in such terms as anger, jealousy, repentance, excitable love, vengeance, and so on. Using such descriptions of God, even if they can be anchored in the Bible, is like throwing mud on an ermine cloak. So too is it considered childish, in an adult quite embarrassing, to speak of animals in similar terms. It is as senseless as trying to make a silk purse out of a sow's ear, this giving to animals an exquisiteness of thought and feeling that they simply do not possess. Anthropomorphism is therefore a form of intellectual dishonesty, perhaps conceit, because it makes what is human the standard for describing what is not human. It might be appropriate as a basis for fantasies, like Orwell's intriguing *Animal Farm*, but it is inappropriate as a basis for assessing the mental or emotive abilities of God at one extreme and animals at another.

I will not deny that anthropomorphism can be misused as a descriptive technique for non-human life. It has a certain seduction (I would not say intellectual dishonesty) that lends it appeal for gaining knowledge of beings other than ourselves — namely, the appeal of the knowledge we have of our own lives. But when it gains tyrannical influence over our thinking this seduction must be resisted; to this extent I agree with the above critics. On the other hand, the use of anthropomorphism can also establish a sense of companionship, a feeling of intimacy that binds us closely to non-human life. Martin Heidegger once wrote that language is the shepherd of Being. Among other things he meant that language has the ability to shape new realities within our minds, new patterns of thought. Thus, the use of anthropomorphic language to describe animals (or God) can create either a self-centered and hence distorted knowledge or a relationship of knowledgeable familiarity and comfort whose source is insight into both ourselves and them.

Our culture teaches us to divide so much of what we do into neat little packets. We are asked to adopt a type of Jekyll-Hyde stance toward our activities, behaving according to one set of values in this situation, another set in that situation. To the delicate mind this can create a tension, a divisiveness within that can cause even the most clear-eyed spiritual vision to blur, dim, and go blind. We begin to lose a sense of wholeness to our lives, that the various factors composing our existence, our differing responsibilities, are nonetheless in communion with each other. In place of the peace of mind this communion brings, there begins to emerge within us a rancorous warfare, one pattern of thought against another. It is as if several rather than just one person were inhabiting our minds and lives. The values that guide us in the boardroom, bedroom, living room, and still other places and times are all different. And so we have the businessman who is not only expected but often encouraged to lie and cheat his way "to the top," but whose similar activity toward members of his family would never be tolerated. Or we have the woman who has made a career out of planning weapons of enormous human destruction, yet at home would be horrified at the suggestion she step on a bug. Or the minister who in the pulpit preaches an unswerving compassion toward others, yet in the parsonage or rectory, to display his authority and the dignity of his office, continually berates the efforts of others assisting him. Or the woman who gives herself generously and completely to her husband during the play of their lovemaking, but will not give a dollar to the beggar at her door. The list could go on endlessly, drawing further illustrations from each of our own lives.

I have mentioned the word "salvation." It is an interesting word, and the history of human effort contemplating its meaning, much like the effort contemplating the word "God," is complex, sometimes maddeningly so. To give it as wide a compass as possible, I myself like to lift the word out of the religious context in which it is so frequently embedded, emphasize its origin (from *salus*, meaning health), and so describe salvation as the process that produces healthiness within us. But immediately I would add that healthiness is the result of harmony among the composite parts of an organism, so that these composite parts function not isolated from each other but for the well-being of the whole. Salvation, then, is harmony or wholeness, just as illness now becomes the breaching of this harmony, the result of a fragmentation causing discord, debilitation, and finally, if untreated or untreatable, death.

The above comments, applied to the meaning of salvation for a human body, can be equally applied to the meaning of salvation for a human spirit. Here too health is harmony or wholeness, in particular the achievement of communion among our values. This is why I would say that the individuals previously described, caught in the Jekyll-Hyde trap of independently functioning values, are not saved. But in this judgment recall that I am opposing salvation not to damnation but to illness. This salvation/damnation dichotomy is too often the opposition set up by religious sentiment, and I want no part of it; I don't like the vocabulary and its implied conceptual frameworks. No — the unsaved human spirit is not damned but sick, and healing is in the achievement of integrity, a consistency in values that gives no heed to whether one is in the boardroom, the bedroom, the living room, or any other place or time. Full harmony within the human spirit, like full harmony within the human body, is pervasive. It does not exist only here and there, now and then, but imbues the whole.

I think the situation described above confronts many people when dealing with their attitude toward animals. A rancher I know, for example, has a stallion on whom he bestows the most lavish attention, grooming him fastidiously and feeding him only the finest grains. Yet he brings this very same horse to rodeos for competition in the bronco contests.

Do you know how the handlers get such horses to buck during the bronco riding exhibitions? The nuances vary, but they tie a strap around the animal's hindquarters and then snuggle or loop it around his testicles. At the second the gate of the holding pen is opened one of the handlers clinches the strap as tight as he can in one swift move; after the exhibition another handler on horseback rides up to the bucking animal as quickly as possible and uncinches the strap. If you've seen a rodeo, you're familiar with these maneuvers. The point is that the horse isn't bucking because it is wild — nearly all of them are quite tame — but because it is in the throes of physical agony. I would not say that the rancher who permits this is evil. But I would say that he is spiritually ill, and the illness is the lack of integrity, the failure of wholeness or consistency in the values guiding his behavior. If he *always* treated the animal the way he does in the holding pen he would be evil, just as if he always treated him the way he does on the ranch he would be good. As it is, the man's spirit is simply unwell and needs healing.

∽

I suppose there is no area where the above inconsistency is more apparent than that of animal experimentation. Here it is present not just in individuals but in the law as well. What happens to animals in experimental laboratories is one of those secrets that many prefer remain hidden, like the same attitude regarding what is going on in laboratories designing increasingly effective and accurate nuclear weapons. This is knowledge that many simply prefer not to possess, a gnawing, disturbing knowledge that gives enormous appeal to the ancient maxim that ignorance is bliss. Again, it is a Jekyll-Hyde situation. With one half of our minds we know the generalities of what is happening in these laboratories, nice abstract generalities, while with the other half we steadily refuse knowledge of the specifics — or, having the knowledge forced upon us, we refuse its truth as representing everyday behavior in animal experimentation.

I once saw a film in which a baboon had been tied down to an examining table with her mouth taped shut and various wires attached to her head and chest. Then one of the examiners began hitting the top of her skull with a calibrated hammer. The point of the experiment was to study the effects of cranial concussions. With every two or three blows, the device struck harder, until, after a lapse of about ten minutes, the skull cracked open and the baboon, of course, died. During the whole procedure, despite the restraints and until a merciful unconsciousness intervened, you could see the animal's body stretching and writhing, seeking a freedom from her damnable torture. No narcotics had been given lest they interfere with the results of the experiment. And why was the tape across the mouth used? For the convenience of the experimenters — so they wouldn't be distracted from their task by the animal's screams. All that got through was the sound of muffled sobbing. The Marquis de Sade couldn't have improved upon the script of this film, the cold, analytic tone of the announcer, his dismissal of the animal's pain as unimportant, what I can only describe as his sadism in approving what was happening, encouraging, at the film's end, further research along the same lines.

I have also read of animal experimentation in laboratories that manufacture cosmetics for women. In one experiment chemicals being tested as ingredients in mascara were introduced into the eyes of rabbits to determine their toxicity. In one animal after another burning and blinding occurred — all for the sake of human vanity — and the animal was killed by bludgeoning, slitting its throat, or lethal injection. The body was then incinerated. This type of experimentation is allowed to continue because concerned public protest is inadequately organized and there are no laws to prevent it. For the law, as I said, is inconsistent on this issue. In a state where I once lived, for example, it is a criminal offense to abandon an animal for whose care you have assumed responsibility; and the law is admirably enforced. Yet in this same state there is a medical school where profligate animal experimentation is the order of the day. Yet the law is mostly silent on this matter, its officers refusing to examine, let alone determine the purpose or need for the various experiments. An abandoned animal has a far better chance at survival than any animal entering the doors of this medical school.

I do not wish to be completely negative on this issue. It is true that there are many scientists who are intransigently hardened on the question of animal experimentation; they could care less how the animals are treated. But there are also scientists who are not, sensitive men and women who view animal experimentation as essential to their research but want it carried out with the greatest humaneness possible. In some few places this latter viewpoint has won the day, and sensitivity to an animal's pain controls the contours of experimentation. But in many places it has not, and the barbarity that treats living animals with the same indifference as disposable syringes and cotton swabs continues. It is an ethical mess I am describing here, a perplexity in human values that simply must be confronted.

The key ingredient in clearing this quagmire is, again, sympathy, a kindness and consideration of spirit we direct at all living things. I myself am not yet convinced of the necessity of most, perhaps all animal experimentation, and I am familiar with both the gross and delicately woven arguments to the contrary. In many of them — given the sophisticated technologies of medical research, the advances, for example, in computer graphics and analysis — I detect a too great concern with the easy availability of animals for experimental procedures as well as a nearly obsessive worry about finances. But because there are enough animals to poison, dismember, and slice open, and because their cost is free or negligible, this is surely not sufficient justification for the brutal abuse and death meted out to them daily in experimental laboratories.

If it is, then a cold eye must be cast on the species egotism that undergirds both the approval and performance of such behavior. It is the same cold eye we still must cast on the immeasurably more monstrous horror of the racial egotism that once approved the use of human skin, flayed from poisoned bodies in Nazi concentration camps, to make lampshades.

I do not want to be misunderstood here. I am aware of the claim that there is animal experimentation that is absolutely necessary at certain stages in developing cures for human diseases. Of particular urgency are diseases that can cripple or kill the young. In such cases it may be inappropriate to speak of species egotism and speak rather of species concern. In other words, I will not contend with the idea that a species, like an individual, has an impulse (I'm uncomfortable calling it a right) to do anything necessary to preserve and enhance its continued existence. My contention, when animal experimentation is involved, is with how this impulse is carried out, how the animals are treated, the amount of pain inflicted, whether or not their lives are honored while we engage ways of improving our own. I would rather have us pursue research on animals, say, if needed to cure childhood leukemia than to have that disease continue claiming victims, though I would still want to monitor closely the quest of even this noble goal.

But even when experimentation is done with the utmost honor and care for the animal, with an unqualified concern that the animal not suffer, the animal has still been abused and is often killed as a result of the research. And this is evil; I will not alter this judgment. But it is evil as an expression of what I call biblical tragedy. Many of us are familiar with the better known expressions of Greek tragedy: the tragedy resulting from a so-called fatal flaw within an individual, something that causes him or her, consciously or unconsciously, to act in evil ways. Thus, to cite perhaps the most famous example, it is the ignorance of Oedipus, his fatal flaw of not knowing his parentage, that causes him to marry his own mother. The evil is enormous, breaking the ancient taboo against mother-son incest, and when discovered impels Oedipus to blind himself. Similarly, we find another flaw in the main characters of Shakespeare's remarkable play *Romeo and Juliet* (the best, I think, of his tragedies), where the two lovers die because they have taken literally everything they have been told, especially by their confessor.

Biblical tragedy, on the other hand, occurs whenever the individual is faced with choosing between options, all of which are evil. It is the tragedy that Jesus likely experienced when having to choose between the evil of denying his mission for the sake of safety from his enemies and the evil of facing a premature and tortured death for remaining loyal to this mission. It is a no-win situation, and ethical propriety requires that the individual choose the option least evil. But it is evil nonetheless, and the individual must not lose sight of this fact, trying to bless an evil deed by arguing that all other choices were more heinous (Jesus, then, does not bless his death; he blesses his executioners). Much of the sorrow that fills biblical narratives is due to this situation, and much of the contrition too. In my view it is the same situation, and the same sorrow, that should control the thoughts and feelings of the experimenter on animals.

Some people think that modern science has produced a new age of barbarism. But it is not the scientists who are blamed so much as the technicians and politicians who decide what use to make of the science. A profound illustration is the science that learned to control the energy of the atom and the technology and political concerns that utilized this knowledge in the creation of weapons designed for the gross, perhaps global extinction of living beings. Another would be the science and technological application employed in manufacturing machines that in our culture tempt us toward an increasing physical and mental indolence. For some the benefits accruing from science run a poor second to the malignant possibilities it has unbridled against physical and spiritual well-being. Some of these people hope for a muddle-headed return to an earlier age, forgetting that all human ages are scarred by their peculiar barbarities. Others are more prescient and intelligently disposed, wishing to challenge and defeat these malignant possibilities by articulate and reasoned discourse.

I am not unsympathetic to the above description of a new age of barbarism come upon us. I think sufficient instances of it can be given to cause anyone contemplation. I know there are places in this country where unwanted animals are still killed in vacuum chambers, thirty or forty of them rounded up in a room whose atmosphere is slowly withdrawn, emerging twenty minutes later as corpses with splayed legs and screaming agony etched on their faces. I know there are companies that buy these corpses as components in protein detergents. But I also know that in most places unwanted animals are now killed by painless lethal injections and most companies procure the protein for their detergents synthetically or from plants. So some progress has occurred. It is the hope and task of all who cherish animals to see that such progress not only continues but expands into other areas of animal care as well. The divinity and humanity our language has given animals since ancient days involves us necessarily in both a reverential and protective love for them. Either that, or the language should be altogether abandoned as no longer persuasive, and so sterile and ineffective. Yet at the close of this second chapter, the latter is an option I would hope no one takes.

CHAPTER THREE

~

A Guilty Carnivore

~

In folklore we sometimes come across the image of a self-consuming serpent, or some other animal, who does not have to rely on an external food source to gain its nutrition. When hungry it simply eats a part of itself. This idea, of course, while perhaps causing a certain aesthetic delight (or repulsion), romping around our imaginations and art, cannot be a source for serious thought. It is the result of what I call a "high" mythology (stories that have no anchorage in objective reality) as compared to a "low" mythology (stories that do have such an anchorage). An example of the distinction can be found when comparing the Old Testament story of Jonah surviving three days in the belly of a fish (a high mythology) and the New Testament story about Jesus being raised from the dead after three days in the tomb (a low mythology). I might also add as a further comment that this distinction causes special heartaches for a lot of Christians who wish to assert the objective reliability of all biblical narratives and the immutability of their understanding of these narratives. Frequently I have the impression that these people, unbending conservatives, are trying to deny the very essence of the universe and all that is within it, which is change. They want desperately to believe, say, that Methusaleh actually lived nine hundred years, refusing to accept the fact that the authors of the text were not fools (no human lives that long without death intervening) but ascribed such longevity to Methusaleh as a literary device to indicate, not how long he actually lived, but the extent of his holiness. So, if the self-consuming serpent, like Jonah in the belly of a fish and Methusaleh's age, is a high mythology, we conclude that all living animals must seek their nourishment outside themselves; they must feed on other living things to stay alive.

But the food that animals eat is not only necessary to maintain their existence, it is also a major factor in determining the various physiological forms they take. The hippopotamus is a herbivore, meaning its preferred diet is vegetation, while a leopard is a carnivore preferring other animal flesh. So the teeth of the hippopotamus are contoured for the grinding of plants, those of the leopard for the stabbing and tearing of meat. And because the hippo's food cannot run away, the animal need not be light on its feet, as the leopard must be. I am not saying that the hippo will eat *only* vegetation. If hungry and lucky enough to catch one, it will munch on a monkey, just as the hungry leopard, failing in the hunt, will occasionally eat grasses. But their normal source of food is a critical determinant toward the physical form these and other animals develop. A similar situation may also be said to describe the spiritual as well as physical formation of human beings. If you are a Christian, for example, your spirit will be principally nourished on the New Testament witness to Jesus, though this can be supplemented by studies of psychology, philosophy, poetry, political theory, and so on. If, however, you begin nourishing your spirit principally on a source other than the New Testament (Marxism and Buddhism attract many), then the contours of your spirit must inevitably change and you become something other than a Christian — just like the physical contours of hippos would gradually change if they became increasingly carnivorous or leopards if they began to prefer eating plants.

Physiologically human beings are classified as omnivores (some also classify themselves this way spiritually), along with such other groups of animals as bears and pigs. This means that our normal diet spans the gamut between plants and animals. It is why we can equally enjoy a spinach salad, a chilled pineapple, chocolate bars, a filet mignon, or a poached salmon. Again, this fact is a determinant of physiology, explaining in part the teeth we have, our stomach and the acids it secretes, the particular shape and functions of our intestinal tract. Omnivores such as ourselves therefore have a clear survival advantage over other animals with more restricted diets. Pandas have a preferred if not sole diet consisting of a certain species of bamboo. Unfortunately this bamboo flowers and dies in mass quantities at regular intervals over the geography pandas inhabit. When this occurs, many pandas die. It is a recurring threat to survival that omnivorous humans do not have to face. Add to this the fact that we have also mastered cooking, making available many food sources we would otherwise have difficulty digesting, and the nourishment that can sustain us becomes truly catholic.

Paleoanthropologists tell us that our early human ancestors were hunter-gatherers. We moved around, following the herds and plucking berries, fruits, and grains while we went. With the emergence of settled agriculture and the domestication of favored animals for meat supplies, we simply made things easier for ourselves, cutting out the travelling and making possible a home, or at least a home base. In another sense, of course, this emergence led to deleterious results. Attempting to steal or protect a home led to individual violence; for the same reasons groupings of kindred homes led to clan violence, then to tribal violence, and finally to the violence between nation states with which we are all familiar. But all along this sorry path we did our best to secure reliable sources of plants and animals to eat. When this failed, we sometimes ate each other.

I mentioned in chapter one that there once were tribal groups whose members practiced rituals of apology before slaughtering an animal for food. Perhaps there still are such groups; I don't know. In most instances the motive for the apology was one or both of the following: a plain respect for the animal as a living being and a reverence for the animal's body as the habitat of a deity (or at least the representation of a deity). In such groups, though, there was an intimacy with the surrounding world, a sensitivity to the interrelatedness prevailing between whole varieties of creatures, including humankind, and a direct experience of what the slaughtering of animals involved, which many of us today no longer possess. Given the limits of the killing techniques available and the participatory nature of many hunts, no member of such groups was likely unaware of the pain endured by an animal being slaughtered. The kindest death they knew came from a savage blow to the head, something difficult to perform, however, unless the animal has first been captured.

I suspect that most of us today, at least in American and European societies, have inured ourselves to the procedures that produce meat on our tables. And we have done so through the deliberate pursuit of ignorance. We don't wish to hear about these procedures, we don't wish to contemplate or discuss them, and above all we certainly don't wish to see them. It is the same ignorance we typically prefer about medical procedures. We just do not want to be witnesses to the blood, bone, and tissue exposed, nor do we find conversations about such things particularly well-mannered. And many physicians, like many slaughterhouse workers, prefer to keep it that way. In many American hospitals it wasn't until recent years that a prospective father was even permitted (if he was willing) to be with his wife at the birth of their new child. Lewis Mumford and others have pointed out the obvious discrepancy: the one animal on Earth most willing to shed the blood of its own kind is the one most repelled by the sight of this same blood.

A fair number of years ago, my age at the time was eleven, I visited a slaughterhouse. The owners had decided on a relocation, and since my father worked for a moving company, he was sent to make a bid. I went with him, not really aware of what I was going to see. When we arrived two men met us. The first offered to escort my father to his office while informing the second to "show the kid around." I didn't like this second man from the instant I saw him. He had one of those faces that invoke immediate distrust in a lad, and more than a little fear. There was something about the eyes, the twist of the mouth that did it. But my dad was encouraging, and so, despite my feelings, I went with the man. My strongest memory of the departing moment on that tour was the overpowering smell of disinfectant in the air, loaded with the scent of pine, cloying enough to choke a horse.

But it wasn't horses we visited; it was cows. The room was quite large and there were perhaps eighteen cows in it. A set of men were on the floor, and as I watched with growing horror and an ugly acid taste growing in my throat, one of the men muzzled and leashed a cow and brought her to the second man, who promptly bashed her on the head with a sledgehammer. I recollect that he hit the cow three times before she died. The opening comment of my chaperone was, "Quite a sight, ain't it?" and then he proceeded to say that sometimes, if the head wasn't wanted, they decked the cow with a single charge from a double-barrelled shotgun. I looked up at him and remember being struck by the way he was licking his lips. He must have guessed that I was quickly going to demand a return to my father and began speaking faster, disjointedly, trying to fill the little time left with all the nightmare images he could.

He told me that at this particular slaughterhouse (which he kept referring to as a "stockyard") they only used shotguns and sledgehammers. He said it usually took two or three whacks with the hammers, sometimes more to dispatch a cow, but almost always only one good blow to kill a lamb. But he knew of other places where the methods were more varied. Sometimes the animals were wire-rigged and electrocuted, sometimes their mouths and nostrils were taped so they would suffocate. At one place he even saw workers who wrestled the calves and lambs to the ground and twisted their necks until broken — though he assured me this wasn't usual; the men only did it now and then to have fun. At another place pigs were slaughtered by throwing them into large vats of water. Trying to swim, each pig slits its own throat with its front feet. On and on he went, until he finally ended by hooking his thumb at one of the cows and said, "That's where your hamburger comes from, boy." I passed out.

When I regained consciousness I was being carried to the first man's office by my father. He quickly concluded his business, and in a short while we were driving home; it was one of the few times I had won the argument about not seeing a doctor. While in the car I relayed everything I could remember, all that the second man had told me. My dad shook his head, saying that the man was wrong, that he was trying to scare me by lying about what happened at slaughterhouses, even though I had seen with my own eyes the truth of part of what the man had said. I sometimes think that at eleven years of age I knew more about the quirkiness of human malevolence than my father ever would. This was a man who died thinking all was well with the world, the same man who grew angry when I brought him a capped jar of fireflies I had caught, took me outside and released them saying, "Never do that again; God loves even these creatures as much as he loves us." A compassionate, enchanting, lovable spirit lived in my dad. God took him too soon from me.

∾

I know a woman who is a strict vegetarian. She refuses to eat any portion of an animal, and so must follow a very careful diet. There are proteins, for example, needed to maintain health and abundantly present in animal flesh that are difficult to procure elsewhere. Her commitment is almost as thorough and sensitive as that of the Buddhist sage who, honoring the principle of non-harm to all animals, wore a mask over his mouth lest he accidentally inhale an insect. She does not wear such a mask, but if she finds a spider or roach scurrying across her kitchen floor, she will diligently seek to catch it in a jar and then release it outdoors in her garden. She is not aggressive in her commitment, never playing the intellectual bully who tries to coerce your own viewpoint. Yet she talks freely and honestly of how she thinks of animals and our need to honor and protect them. She is, I would say, a true daughter of Adam, but never a daughter of Noah.

The reference is to two covenants described in the book of Genesis. The first is made with Adam and permits him to enjoy all "the fruit of the earth" (except, of course, for the tree of good and evil knowledge). The phrase, "the fruits of the earth," means any plant that grows above or below the ground and, by extension, above or below the water. Of all these Adam and his descendents may eat. But the phrase is also clearly implying a prohibition against consuming animals as food; or differently, it is an injunction toward vegetarianism. Perhaps the motive is the ancient reverence for the spirit in animals; perhaps it is a way for those seeing Adam as the father of the race to distinguish themselves from others (we don't eat meat, while the rest of you do); or perhaps it simply represents a dietary aesthetic that found the taste of animal flesh repulsive.

The prohibition, however, may also be expressing the hope for a day when tranquility will prevail between humans and animals and between the animals themselves. It imagines such peace at the beginning of the human story and longs for its eventual resurrection at some future date. This longing is not uncommon in religious and poetic traditions. Isaiah's sweet desire for a time when the lion will lie down with the lamb is not unknown elsewhere; the steady purpose of those who refuse to eat meat is not recent but has an ancient and honorable lineage. The beauty of this peace has mastered the behavior of many toward animals. But in the whole tale of human behavior most have marred it by the nutrition needs of their own bodies, the ease of securing animal flesh to meet these needs, and the general refusal to acknowledge the pain of being slaughtered. The sad fact is that we have no evidence that the covenant with Adam has ever been seriously kept, save by some, among his children.

The second covenant is the one with Noah. After the flood that drowns a wicked humanity, we are told that among the blessings bestowed on Noah and his descendents is the right to enjoy animals as food, provided the blood is first drained from them. It is likely that the author of the narrative embedded this right in his story from the simple awareness that the prohibition in the Adam covenant had been largely ignored in the history of his people. Men and women have always eaten animals; it is as simple as that. And any injunction to the contrary, while perhaps beautiful in theory, is snuffed out by almost universal human practice. The author of the Noah story is a hardboiled realist. A religion must not impose covenant demands on its adherents that the vast majority of them are happily going to ignore. The author of the Exodus cycle has even less sympathy for the Adam covenant. The people not only have the right to eat animals (with a few minor restrictions subsequently imposed), they have a responsibility to do so, at least on that one day when the Exodus is recalled, Passover with its slaughtered lamb.

I do not want to create a bickering atmosphere on this issue. The truth to tell is that I myself still eat meat occasionally. I find myself enjoying it less and less, and hence its increasingly reduced place in my diet. The flavor and succulence of a well-prepared steak still appeals, the delight to the palate of nicely sauced veal is still there. But it is the idea of the animal that is causing a growing repulsion, bred, born, reared, and killed solely to end up in a human stomach. I used to find an excuse in the fact that the animal was dead and butchered anyway, but this flimsy-headed rationale didn't last; it was too self-serving, too unconcerned with the butchering and the flippant or studied indifference of many to the reason why animals are alive. No — the only reason I still eat animals occasionally is that I like the taste, or sometimes, though less influentially, I don't wish to inconvenience or offend a host. There is nothing more than these prideless motives to explain why I have not yet removed animals, not even the mammals, completely from my diet. And I feel myself a partner, therefore, in St. Paul's confession that "I do not do the things I should, while doing those I should not."

In a couple of my previous books I noted that the word "maturity" comes from an old Indo-European verb, *matur*, meaning to cut or trim. Its usual context is agriculture and its definition captures the process of pruning a plant to assure more robust fruition or flowering. But like many words, the meaning of this one can be taken out of its original or typical context and applied elsewhere. So in many languages today it means not just a technique in field or garden but in the human spirit as well. Maturity is the result of a willingness to rid ourselves of anything that might inhibit or prevent the most fruitful and enriching results of our spiritual growth. In the early years of life — say, to encourage virtue and diminish vice — this interior pruning is done for the child by others. But as the years go by we are expected to take on more and more of this task for ourselves, at least in any good society that does not encourage infantilism or childishness in the comportment of its adults.

I've made the above remarks to indicate that I need further growth in the commitment to the care of animals, that work can be done to assure this commitment is more thoroughgoing, that I need not utilize animals as food. What I am *not* saying is that the spiritual vision proposed here regarding our relationships to animals is the only mature one. There are others; I myself especially admire those of St. Francis and St. Seraphim of Sarov, Stephen Clark, John Cobb, John Hick, C. S. Lewis, Andrew Linzey, Jürgen Moltmann, Tom Regan, and Albert Schweitzer, to name just a handful.* But I want to emphasize that mine is one among them and is worthy of consideration. It is in this mutual consideration of ideas, after all, that we grow intellectually, finding cause to maintain our own particular viewpoint or reasons to refine, alter, or prune it. The atmosphere of such exchange must not become rancorous; this inevitably changes the dialogue between the partners into a series of self-assertive monologues. What is needed, rather, is graceful, courteous, and persuasive speech.

The vegetarian friend I mentioned earlier conducts such dialogues, and from her and others sharing a like viewpoint, plus personal reflection of my own, I have learned much about why they confine their diets. Sheer waste of food is one of the reasons, a notorious commonplace especially in America. I've talked to a man who picks up the canned or bagged refuse in my neighborhood, and his enduring attitude is one of complete perplexity at the amounts and quality of food people throw away uneaten, especially the meat. Any stroll among restaurant tables, where the price of the food and its preparation is always higher, often considerably so, than eating at

---

* Selections from the writings of most of these persons can be found in *Animals and Christianity: A Book of Readings*, edited by Andrew Linzey and Tom Regan (New York: Crossroad, 1988), and an analysis of their various viewpoints in Andrew Linzey, *Christianity and the Rights of Animals* (New York: Crossroad, 1987).

home, would reveal the same thing. Uncommon is the plate taken away that does not still have food on it. I once thought that such observations indicated a people so fearful of being considered poor that their protest was this prodigal squandering. Now I think that for many it is simply the result of the extravagant abundance of food in this society and the indifference toward its uneaten disposal this abundance has encouraged. We have created an ethic of waste.

Another reason is the enormous amounts of grain, of fine quality and in situations of controlled feeding, an animal will consume before it is slaughtered. This grain used to put a delicious roast on the tables of the affluent could make hundreds, if not thousands of loaves of bread to put on the tables of the poor. The principle that comes into play here, as it does with the first reason, derives from the implicit mandate of Jesus, confirmed in the morality promoted by similar great teachers, that you must give of your excess to those who do not have enough to maintain their health and well-being. You do not channel this excess into the creation of luxuries such as expensive meats when there are people who do not have even the necessities of decent nutrition. It is a beautiful principle ignored by many — and, if the reports are true regarding the overburdened greed of our new generation of young adults, it will continue to be ignored.

Still another reason one might offer to recommend the vegetarian's credo is an abhorrence of the ideology of violence pervading so much of our culture. We see this violence everywhere, streets, television, newspapers, our neighbors' or our own homes. It has become an expected, if dreaded, presence in our lives. Sadly, a typical response is to cope with this violence by hardening ourselves to it. As a result many people carry guns in their clothes, or hidden in the glove compartments of their cars, or stashed away in their bedside tables, and they walk warily down nighttime streets, taut with the approach of each passer-by. If our culture is imbued with an ethic of waste, it is equally influenced by an ethic of violence, a pornography of violence as some have termed it. Underlying this ethic is an acceptance of "things as they are," the option for ease described in a previous chapter while the option for actualizing the more difficult possibility of practicing harmony among ourselves, or at least non-violence, is neglected. And I have already noted how this violence we do to ourselves is expressed in even more unbridled and demented ways in the violence we do to animals, including the violence of the slaughterhouse.

The fourth and final reason (final, that is, for our discussion here) has to do with pursuing ideals. The English word "ideal" comes from the Greek *eidolon*, which means any object of beauty that radically affects one's behavior. It is the portrait that causes a man to become a painter, the poem that turns a woman into a poet, the mercy of the saint that seduces the spiteful bully into practicing forgiveness. Ideals are objects of beauty that influence our behavior because we perceive them as critical in defining the meaning we wish our lives to enjoy. But there is a catch to them, something that an achievement-oriented individual (like many in our culture, with what I call their "get-it" mentality) has difficulty accepting — namely, ideals can never be fully possessed, they can only be pursued. Our man, our woman, our spiteful bully will never become perfect in the practice of their art, literature, or forgiveness. So it is with the person who finds an ideal, something beautiful to act upon, in the practice of reverence for all living things.

What this means is that if our lives are made worthy by the ideals guiding us, if we are blessed by the fervor marking our pursuit of them, then this blessing can only be in the striving, not the achievement, of our ideals. It is the passion, not the success, characterizing our lives that can make of them also objects of beauty. Darwin speaks eloquently about the struggle *for* existence. The great Spanish philosopher and poet Miguel de Unamuno speaks just as eloquently about the struggle *of* existence. By this he means the pain, frustrations, and setbacks, the desire to give up and rest easy involved in the chase for beauty. To this the encouragement must always be: it is the chase that matters, not the winning, because beauty is always more swift than we, always just a little out of reach. To honor all living things, to bless the beasts and struggle toward the full acceptance of the grace of their presence in creation, possesses such beauty.

∽

A woman lives down the street from me who treats her pet dog like a person. She has given him a personal name and refuses to use impersonal pronouns when describing him in conversation; the dog is never "it" but always "he" or "him." I suppose all of us do this who have pets, but few whom I know do it with her intensity or extent of application. For she refuses to treat impersonally any living thing, even the small rodents and insects who have made for themselves a pleasure dome of her garden. Knowing my education as a theologian, she once asked if I thought that, along with us, God would raise all the animals from the dead on "that fine day." She had mentioned to me before her concern about what she called the "silly" selfishness of human beings who wanted to hoard just for themselves all God's blessings and loving care. Not to appease her, but because I believe it — and for much the same reason as her comment on our silly selfishness — I said yes.

I prefer (though it doesn't often happen on this issue) to avoid arguments about whether or not animals are persons. It all depends on how you define what a person is — and the thick confusion of our civil laws on animal rights shows just how varied these definitions can be. The same can be said about the discussions that once raged in this country over the legal status of slaves, and elsewhere, especially in much earlier times, of women and children, today of unborn fetuses. While I am not usually a devotee of science-fiction, a remarkable illustration of this confusion can be found in the excellent novel by Roger MacBride Allen, *Orphan of Creation* (New York: Baen Books, 1988), which deals specifically with the legal confusion regarding the question whether or not a surviving colony of australopithecines, hominid primates long considered extinct, are persons protected by civil law. However, I do think we have a right to use words establishing our distinctness from the rest of the world around us. I will not deny this privilege, therefore, to anyone who, for whatever reason, wants to say that only human beings are persons (though in an act of intellectual largesse, he or she might also be willing to extend the term to God). I can always take solace in Shakespeare's haunting *Romeo and Juliet*, with its famous rhetorical question, "What's in a name?"

But the solace never lasts. And it doesn't last because words are important; as I said earlier, language possesses creative power. One of the most potent of these words is "person" — because for many it establishes in the mind a whole array of claims and prerogatives that, if only human beings are persons, belong to nothing else alive. It is when this type of thinking begins, and because of the wrong behavior it can produce, that I would not be uncomfortable endowing all life with personhood. I would depart, in other words, from a long Christian tradition that asserts that only human beings have rights within creation, to use it as their own, including, among others, Origen, Aquinas, Luther, Calvin, and, of course, Karl Barth. This is not to deny differences in our response to various forms of life. We cannot relate the same way to a butterfly as we do to a pet cat, nor to the cat the way we do to another human being. The abilities and potentialities of each partner are radically distinguishable. But in all cases an attitude of wonder wedded to kindness, honor bleached of condescension and indifference, is the needed practice. In my judgment this practice is not virtue, doing the good beyond what is required of us; it is a responsibility.

A similar power of words is present in our taxonomy, the way we divide all living things into various families, classes, genera, species, and subspecies. We sometimes think that once we have slotted given life-forms into the appropriate category, with greater or lesser proximity to our own (*homo sapiens sapiens*), this automatically establishes the extent of our respect and responsibility toward them, the degree of our attentive care. So while many would not hesitate crushing to death with their foot a spider (of the class Arachnida), few would be so thoughtless about the life of a dog (of the class Mammalia). Yet one could suggest that if we trace the beginnings of life back far enough, to its originating source when (for whatever reason) matter became animate, then it is perhaps not too far-fetched to consider all living things as only variable yet related subspecies of this source. This, however, would cause such massive changes in terminology, coupled with radical alterations in our definitions, that even beginning the task now seems highly unlikely, and to many, no doubt, equally as foolish.

When Job was suffering his worst, the advice of his friends was to examine how he was thinking about his fate. It did no good to lament, complain, scream to heaven unreasoned, inarticulate responses to his pain and loss. They even offered particular patterns of thought he might pursue as possible rationales for why God was treating him in such a seemingly cruel way. Of course, Job had already been thinking, diligently and in detail, and had already proposed to himself the options his friends suggested — yet still he could find no adequate explanation for God's behavior. But no matter how we might pity Job, or how irritating, even petulant some of the statements of his friends might strike us, we can recognize that their basic counsel was wise. It matters enormously how we think about what happens to us, or about what we are doing. It is this thought that makes us active participants in our destiny, what we become, rather than mere playthings of present circumstances or future possibilities we never seriously address.

When I think about consuming animals as food, my mind

does a dance. It is slow at first, but then builds in tempo and rhythm. I realize that the animal eaten has become part of us, not in a passing fashion but somehow permanently. I look to current science and discover that this might well be so, that portions of everything we ingest make a home within us through a mixture of molecules, atoms, subatomic particles. As long as we are alive, something of all those animals remains present and active in the tiny composite elements of our bodies. And even after we die they do not disappear. As we blend increasingly into the environment from which we came, they are with us, sharing our own metamorphosis into something else. This is not mystagogy, though it may sound like it. My words are only a recognition of what I take to be the fundamental assertion of the first law of thermodynamics — that all that exists is never completely annihilated. Recognizing old forms in the new transformations is not what's intriguing here, but rather the thought that everything endures.

Perhaps the above remarks can form one basis for a description of resurrection from the dead, honoring, for example, one part of the ancient Christian tradition that resurrection fundamentally involves transformation — though recognizing, too, that what this transformation involves has a wandering, altering, sometimes conflict-ridden history in Christian thought. But we also know that science is often obliged to change its theories, even its so-called laws, on the basis of new observation and experimentation. And then there are the corresponding questions. Do atomic or subatomic particles endure indefinitely? When matter is transformed into energy, does a portion of it disappear, so that eventually there will be no matter in the universe? Is energy eternal, so that what things are, including ourselves, will ultimately exist as simply the presence of energy? On and on the questions go, exciting yet somewhat scary, giving us endless supplies of intellectual knots to untie and making us aware that our knowledge about anything, and the decisions we make based upon it, is never final but only varyingly tentative.

When I contemplate the brutal slaughter of animals for food, not just by human beings but in fact mainly by other animals, the poetry of Tennyson about "Nature red in tooth and claw" scourges my mind and makes me deeply sad. Is the feeding of others the sole purpose of all this pain? To what destiny other than a digestive tract are these lives being directed? I take some consolation in the science telling me of the possibility that everything endures indefinitely in some form. But more enchanting is the idea of Alfred North Whitehead: that there is a God, and all that has ever existed continues living, though only in God's memory. More provocative, and for me more appealing, is the idea that there is indeed a God, and that in a time determined by this God's good will, all that ever existed will be raised to new life, touching, communicating, enjoying a peace with each other that will not end because there is no more death. I say this because I use as one of my criteria for assessing theological propositions or faith statements (such as, only human beings will be raised by God from the dead), the inquiry, "What does it require me to say about God?" If the proposition or statement, like the foregoing one, requires me to say something about God I don't wish to (on the basis, pre-eminently, of my understanding of the gospels), I look for alternate ways of thinking. In the nineteenth century Schleiermacher spoke of the "cultured despisers of religion." Perhaps this idea appealing to me, that all living things will be raised from the dead, most definitely a religious one, will be despised by some — a high mythology as I previously described this, unanchored in any objective reality, a hope excusable only in childish minds. To this I say that a believer must be wary before putting constraints on either the abilities or mercy of God.

The more we consume animals as food, the more those animals become a part of us, contributing to our entire physiology. A receptive mind, given to metaphor, might say that at a certain point the animals have become a sufficient part of us so that continuing to eat them begins to take on the character of cannibalism. I like this saying. And to those who say contrariwise that the *first* thing on their minds when they are eating a well-prepared piece of meat is the pleasure it gives, and the *last* thing the animal killed to give this pleasure, I would take another saying and apply it to this type of thinking in the hope that one day it will change — for on the highest authority we are told that the first shall be last, and the last first.

CHAPTER FOUR

❦

The Healing Kind

❦

For a number of years when I was a younger man, in my early twenties, I used to visit a county home every week. It wasn't a place for the aged or physically infirm, as most of the residents were in their forties or fifties and reasonably healthy. It was for people who more or less had given up on life, unable or unwilling to provide themselves decent shelter, food, clothing, the common needs of ordinary life. Many of them had children, and much of their psychological unrest was due to the fact that these children would not give them any time or attention, not visiting or even calling them. The women would often start crying when telling such things, the men would stop short and just stare at the floor. Every week I had to steady myself for the visit, knowing that afterward I too would sometimes start crying. It was the women especially who unnerved me, as if their whole lives had become little more than a wait for a loving embrace.

One of these women was named Greta. I liked her enormously. She was one of the very few residents who had a room to herself, a fairly large one at the corner of the building. She was an independent-minded woman, warm, affectionate, and liked by all, who suffered regularly from severe depression. During these times she wanted no visitors, would scarcely eat, and spent most of her day in directionless pacing of her room or the corridors. A twitch would develop in her neck and she would continuously rub her hands together. So worried would I become at such times that one day I spoke with the home's administrator, a compassionate man always willing to give his attention to the care of those he called his "family." During that chat he made a suggestion that I immediately liked, an insightful suggestion, I thought, that needed no argumentation, no further thought about its wisdom. The next time I visited Greta I brought her a kitten.

I had never seen greater happiness on someone's face than when I placed the kitten in Greta's lap. She began stroking him, cooing and speaking softly, forgetful that I was even in the room. In later weeks it was clear to everyone that the kitten had become the center of her life. It was not that she ignored the other residents; in fact, her care for them grew even greater. To everyone's delight her times of depression also decreased in regularity and severity, until disappearing altogether. We all knew it was the kitten's presence working on her, a presence shared by all since Greta asked, and the administrator approved, permission to allow the animal to roam free through the building, though Greta was always nearby. About two years later Greta died, victim to her weak, loving heart. For some reason no one ever understood, her kitten died four hours later.

There is a growing body of data drawn from psychological and psychiatric studies that indicates the healing presence of pet animals for certain mental dysfunctions. Gerontological studies are also revealing the consoling, sometimes energizing effects the presence of animals has on otherwise lonely, aged people. Now and then I smile when I read such reports. For generations those who have nurtured animals, especially pet animals, could have told anyone of these same effects; the blessing of scientific studies about them is hardly needed. I watched Greta's feelings metamorphose into even finer, more exquisite expressions of her spiritual life because of her kitten. I have seen the same thing in others, friends who have grown in kindness and tolerance, students of mine showing a more mature sense of responsibility, neighbors now speaking who previously shared no communication. There is no doubt in my mind about the therapeutic, healing value of the presence of animals in our lives — just as I could say of flowers or the warming sun when winter passes.

Much of this therapeutic influence comes from our tactile experiences with animals, touching and being touched by them. So while I know, for example, that sitting in a darkened room watching a lit aquarium of tropical fish can be a soothing, relaxing experience, especially if accompanied by Mahler or Chopin, it is more limited in its enduring effects than the sight *and* feel of a favored dog or cat, even the moving warm fur of a gerbil or the feathers of a parrot. From the moment we are born there is a delight in touching and being touched by the living that is never surpassed, as studies of infant melancholy and withdrawal demonstrate when this touching is sparse or absent. Even as the years go by, and our culture, especially our religion, teaches us to restrain this delight, it doesn't disappear; it only becomes frustrated. What a woman or man recently widowed wants above all else is not to be told comforting words but to be held in someone's arms.

There are some "purists" in animal care organizations who say that animals should be kept only for their own sakes — that any positive effects such keeping has for human beings should not be a factor in determining the placement of the animals. I disagree with this stance by citing the single example of Greta. It is true her kitten had enormously beneficial effects on her. But equally as true is the fact that she had similar effects on him, with her daily attentive care and nourishment. The pleasing companionship worked both ways, not just one. I also disagree with a man I know who works for an animal adoption agency. He refuses to allow anyone to take just a single animal, always insisting on a minimum of two. His argument is that animals need the company of their own kind. But many people want only one animal, and so walk away unhappy, taking none. This is not a service to the animals, since at least one of them might have been given a decent home, with or without a species partner. Nor is it a service to the inquirers, since their lives might have been more richly blessed by the presence of the pet animal they were seeking.

The positive effects of the presence of an animal are not confined only to the psychologically hurt or harmed. These same effects can be seen even in those who are generally healthy of mind, not usually battered about by a conflict of desires or values, by frustration and a personal history that reads like a case study devoted to failure. Even those spared the consuming power of such conflicts must still get through a life often marred by disappointments and a lack of pleasure, needing at such times consolation and a feeling of being accepted. None of us is exempt from these experiences. Hamlet speaks of an outrageous fortune that penetrates all our lives, causing a distraught spirit and the condemning conscience that tells us we have not been a success at what we have done. And Macbeth, more severely, speaks of human life as a tale told by an idiot. These judgments: to varying degrees, with greater or lesser regularity, they haunt each of us.

Success at what we do is a pre-eminent value in our culture, a bitch-goddess, someone once said, who seeks to control the parameters of our entire existence. Suicides occur, marriages are broken, friendships demeaned and sullied because of lack of success. Yet animals do not value our successes. They do not ask how swollen our bank account is, how wide our fame, how plundering our sexual conquests, how powerful we are over human lives. They do not ask because they do not care, they cannot care about such matters, any more than God does. And I am speaking here of all animals, not just favored pets. I am speaking of the Persian sleeping at the foot of your bed, the killdeer with its plaintive cry during midnight flights, the frisky pup who worships your presence, the manta ray gracing the waters of a coral sea. When you wish a sure comfort in your distress, seek the company of animals, should there be no true human friend at hand.

The healing, therapeutic presence of animals has at least four components (currently I can think of four; I'm sure there may be others). I am speaking now especially of pet animals. First, there is the sense of commitment that the animal can create in us. The word "commitment" comes from the Latin prefix *con-* plus the verb *mittere*, which originally meant to connect, later, to send. The prefix functions as an intensive, so that *con-mittere* means to connect thoroughly, completely, in a mutually influential fashion. A commitment, in other words, is something you are connected to in a binding way that presides over your behavior. It gives purpose to life, goals to achieve, a sense of knowing what you must do; in a sense it is somewhat like a vow, freely chosen yet channeling your freedom in particular directions. As I said above, a pet animal can draw this commitment from us, for some people (perhaps sadly) in ways that nothing else can quite match. I once met an old woman in a park feeding pigeons. She said she did it every day, without failure, no matter what the weather held. I asked her why. She said the pigeons had never abandoned her, like people had.

Second, there is the sense of accomplishment that the animal can create in us. The products of our care, the healthy, active, well-groomed animal, full of joy at our returns, morose while we are absent, demonstrates the achievement of an affective bond that pleases us. So, too, our delightful feelings of acceptance by the animal, shown in soft purrings, leg rubbing, scurrying to the perch's point nearest us, demonstrate not just what we have accomplished in the animal, but what the animal has accomplished in us. A mutuality of good-will is achieved that injects our existence with feelings of having done something admirable, even beautiful. In times of failure, when our accomplishments seem so few and far between, these feelings can put an end to the dripping away of our self-respect. We find echoed in our minds the sentiment of Albert Schweitzer, and of an old woman feeding pigeons in a park, that animals can contribute to our feelings of worth as much as we allow.

Third, and related to the above, animal care can create an awareness of responsibility. This is first of all a responsiveness to the animal's needs, and then responsiveness to its corresponding displays of pleasure or attention. The feeling of one's obligation here, the sense of duty implied, can lift a human spirit depressed by the thought that nothing matters, or that one's behavior has become kaleidoscopic, a mad-hatter's dance down life wherein nothing one does has purpose or lasting intelligence. An awareness of responsibility, even for the well-being of just one small animal, can clear this confusion and its attendant depression — if not entirely, often sufficiently enough to provide a catalyst for assuming even more responsibility for and within one's existence. The chronically irresponsible individual (whether the source is youth, forms of mental disturbance, mere indolence, or whatever) must not be left alone but instead must be encouraged to engage as effectively and as much as possible life in his or her surrounding world.

Fourth, and largely as a result of the previous three components, animal care can create a feeling of gratitude within the individual. The happiness that one's commitment, accomplishment, and responsibility elicit can seem a gift, something attending one's care that is felt as undeserved — a bonus, if you will, to the time and effort expended toward the animal's nurturing. In the human spirit sensitive to these feelings, thankfulness emerges as the appropriate response. It is the same thankfulness we feel whenever a therapeutic procedure has worked, producing an alleviation (or at least a lessening) of some physical or psychological distress we are experiencing. Healing can come in a variety of ways, through surgeries and medications, rest, prayer, intelligent dialogue, the serenity of a relaxed journey. One of these ways is the practice of care toward another life dependent on you for its well-being and the mutually grateful response this care brings to pass.

∾

In Buddhist folklore there is a story about a monk and a scorpion. While on a walk one day the monk came to a pond and, sitting down, began examining its contents. In the course of this he spotted a scorpion on the water, which, because he was a good Buddhist monk and honored the principle of non-harm to all living things, he picked up. The scorpion promptly stung him. He put the animal down, thinking his responsibility was acquitted, and the scorpion immediately scurried back onto the water. So the monk picked the animal up again, and again was promptly stung. This went on several more times until, we are told, the scorpion decided that the monk was stubborn, that there was no sense in trying for the water again, and so ran off into the surrounding grass. The monk, at last satisfied, got up and continued his walk.

This little story is designed to illustrate the unqualified compassion of the good Buddhist. Even after being stung several times by the fearsome scorpion, the monk persists in keeping the animal out of harm's way. There is a diligence to the compassion here, and a familiarity, a certain at-homeness with animals that I have always found very lovely. The story tells us that if the presence of animals can provide therapeutic assistance in our lives, we can provide the very same thing in their lives. I only wish I could draw a similar story from the origins of my own religious tradition, but I can't. Save for a few passing references to animals in his teaching and the likelihood of his disapproval of animal sacrifice, Jesus — the Jesus at any rate described in the gospels — appears to have shown them little *direct* concern. But if there is some truth in Nietzsche's exaggerated claim that the true spirit of Jesus has been reaffirmed only once in Christian history, in the life of Francis of Assisi, then perhaps Jesus himself was far more attentive to animal life than our records indicate. For Francis, we know, had an abiding and compassionate love for animals.

The Buddhist monk who cherished the scorpion would be shocked at some of the ways, common ways, we treat animals. I wonder what he would think, for example, if instead of strolling by a pond he strolled by the enclosures in American zoos. In some of these zoos he would undoubtedly be pleased. The animals are given sufficient space, clean and adequate shelter, excellent food, and conscientious medical care. While they might well prefer the freedom of their natural habitats, the security of their enclosures and the reliability of their keepers, produces healthy animals. The monk would say the principle of non-harm was at work in such places. We might say, in a more complicated vocabulary, that the therapeutic environment of these zoos assured a well-balanced animal psychology, with some deviants to be expected — the same as we would find in nurturing well-disposed human environments.

In other zoos our monk would not be nearly as pleased. I myself have been to several zoos where the environment is not only non-therapeutic but openly antagonistic toward the animals' proper care. In one the wading pool for the hippo was so narrow and shallow that the animal could not immerse completely in the water nor turn around. To get out he had to walk backward. Consequently he never went into the pool, a critical distress in the life of a hippo. In another the monkey cages were filthy, excrement and uneaten rotting food everywhere, the bodies of the animals covered with mange. In this same zoo the large cats were kept in cages in an exhibition building all the time; there were no outdoor enclosures for them. In still another I saw a keeper with a thick plank of wood beating a baby elephant on the head for knocking over a pail of water. Zoos can be bewitching places, filled with enough wonders to delight even the roughest human spirit. But some are more like madhouses, with fright, abuse, neglect, and contempt souring the very air.

When confronted with such observations, zookeepers frequently have a legitimate complaint insofar as their finances are strictly limited and controlled. This accounts for the inadequacy of the enclosures, the poor quality of food and medical care, and the problems with low-salaried personnel. Many zoos are dependent for money on private benefaction or a slight fraction of city or state taxes; most of them also charge a moderate entrance fee. Yet these sources are often not sufficient to provide healthy, stressless environments for the animals. And while zoos give pleasure to most who visit, many remain unaware of the costs involved in upkeep — or, aware of these costs, they take their pleasure and run. The animals meanwhile are left to their truncated lives, morose, alienated, badly fed, and waiting to die. It can be nothing but a cause for shame to any population that permits the existence of such places within the borders of its town or city. And a similar shame should also describe our attitude toward the intensive farming of animals, when hundreds or thousands are often kept most of their lives in pens or cages that prohibit lying down, turning around, or even stretching. Sometimes these enclosures have angled or slatted floors that cause swollen or broken feet, they are rarely washed, and, along with such other practices as castration and de-beaking, the animals are kept continually dark to diminish restlessness and aggression.

The inadequacy of many of our zoos and animal farms pales, however, when compared to what we do to the natural environments of animals, and thus to the animals within them. Whenever we build carelessly or indiscriminately we irreparably damage the habitats of many forms of life. And imagine what happens to living things in the vicinity of one of our bomb tests, especially nuclear but also so-called conventional bombs. The testers of these bombs and those who construct our buildings may blithely dismiss such thoughts as irrelevant, or the death of the animals involved as a necessary expedient, an unimportant by-product of progress. But the sensitive mind does not make such judgments. Attuned to the beauty of animal life, knowing the therapeutic value it possesses for the distressed human spirit, the sensitive mind wishes to repay this beauty in kind by securing the safety of its givers from human threat.

But the sensitive mind also knows that we must have buildings to live in, we must have shelters and places of relaxation; sadly, too, we are still policy-driven to test our bombs and weapons. At this point we have re-entered the arena of biblical tragedy previously described. We find ourselves forced to do one evil (no matter how carefully we build or test, animals and their habitats still get destroyed) in order to avoid what we perceive as a greater evil. Yet this arena is not the place from which we observe, for example, the massive deforestation still occurring in the jungles of Brazil. To bolster national pride as well as individual pocketbooks, untold numbers of animals — insects, birds, river dwellers, even primates — are being obliterated by the assault of ingenious human machines, with the money earned fattening the wealth of the rich even more while the poor receive little if any aid. Whole species have been extinguished. Even more alarming, if such a thing is imaginable, is the death of so many plants that oxygenate our atmosphere, depleting the single most important element in the very air we breathe. This action is not only wrong; it is stupid, some would say insane.

But we continue to molest animals not only for reasons of national pride and economy but also as an outlet for hostility. We treat the land and its non-human inhabitants as a playground to vent our aggression. It is one thing to hunt animals when food is needed; it is quite another to use them for mere target practice. And the bigger or more wily the target is, the better. You see, the song of those dying baby turtles still lingers in my mind, like the ancient church canticles I sang in my youth. So jaguars, tigers, ostriches, alligators are shot for the mere fun of it, a further bonus gained if their pelts or feathers can be used to drape a human frame. Or a rhinoceros is shot and the only thing taken from its body is the horn, because the foolishness of some insists it functions as an aphrodisiac. I have seen men in Montana shoot terrified jackrabbits just to kill something; I have seen films of men doing the same with baboons in Africa. And then, at the end of their lethal play, they drink beer and congratulate each other. These are not the kind of men who would appreciate the idea that it is far more satisfying to be intoxicated on God than being so on beer. Dante put nine circles in hell; he should have put one more, somewhere between the wasters and the murderers, for people who treat animals like this.

The ecology of marine life is intricately, marvelously balanced, as most ecologies are. And it takes very little to disturb this balance — say, a rise in water temperature of one or two degrees or a slight alteration in chemical content. In the vicinity of the outflow pipes from a nuclear generating plant, most if not all river or ocean animals must either quickly depart or die because of the increased water heat; if the living return it is only because they have adapted to the new environment. And no animals survive in the near vicinity of toxic sewage or a leaking oil tanker, unless they are indeed quick to get away. There are some people stubborn or ignorant enough to deny even the clarity of the noonday sun. It is clear that in behavior like indiscriminate building, deforestation, hunting, and the release of energy producing by-products into the environment (think here also of automobile, home, and factory exhaust), we are doing something that not only kills non-human life, but seriously threatens the dignity and value, even the existence of our own. There is no therapeutic or healing worth in this behavior for any living creature. There is only the dismal forecast of disasters that have already begun.

∽

It is a standard exhortation in biology nowadays to speak of the Earth as an ecosystem. This is meant to discourage any judgment of the planet as a mere congeries of varying parts that can be studied independently. Or differently, it is meant to discourage a too zealous reductionism when attempting to understand this home of ours. The Earth is a whole, a communion of interlocking parts, in one sense a single living entity. The richness of thought and images this idea contains is remarkable. One of these, which we touched on in an earlier chapter, is that any understanding of the Earth must therefore be organic — that reductionism, while needed to improve our understanding of the individual components populating the Earth's ecosystem, more specifically its biosystem, is never sufficient. This understanding of the differing bits and pieces comprising the Earth's physiology must be put into the context of a wider meaning, an encompassing viewpoint designed to lead to appreciation and respect for the whole of life. In a marvelously indirect way, I think, the author of Genesis is making the very same point when he has God say (though the context is often interpreted as a curse) that all life comes from dust and to dust it shall all return. This dust: to the biblical author it is the simplest of matter, the equivalent of the subatomic units our modern science has discovered. Left alone, without benefit of resurrection, the fate of a human being, the most complex of creatures, is thus a circle, from simplicity to simplicity, but in between capable beyond every other animal of formulating thankful and motivating visions of the relationships between all living things.

But if the Earth is indeed an organism and our task is to produce a vision appreciating the entirety of this organism, then one essential portion of this task must center on the issue of health. We all know how health is achieved and maintained in ourselves and, so far as we know, all other living things. It is the result of the balanced interrelationships of the individual members composing the organism. More imaginatively put, health is the product of the peaceful co-existence within and among the societies — like the respiratory, circulatory, and digestive societies — that compose a living body. It follows from the symbolic functions of a body's members (from the Greek *symbolein*, meaning to unify, to bring and work together) as opposed to their diabolic functions (from the Greek *diabolein*, meaning to break apart or sunder or set at odds with each other). So we can conclude that health is always symbolic in its manifestations, illness always diabolic.

If the Earth is indeed a living entity, then its health also depends upon peaceful co-existence within and between its differing societies. We do not need to slip into ancient metaphors here; we need not speak of the Earth, say, as our mother, though I myself am not adverse to such vocabulary. It is the idea underlying these metaphors that is important: how the individual members or societies of an organism behave affects the behavior of other members or societies in the organism, now in service to health, now producing illness. We all have common enough experiences of this. It is the mouth that has eaten unhealthy food, but it is the belly that suffers; or again, it is the kneecap that has been broken, but it is the whole leg that throbs with pain. There is an intimacy of relationships here that cannot be denied, a communion or co-existence intelligently ignored only in the diagnostic procedures of biological study concerned with the performance of distinct body parts. In a playful mood of thought we might say that if a body spoke to its entire membership it would affirm, "We are all in this together."

If the Earth is a living entity, then how its differing societies relate to each other will therefore be an essential ingredient to its health. One of these societies is composed of the animals, another of human beings. Obviously I am not saying that these two societies alone compose Earth's life, nor even that either represents a more blessed presence in this life than others. All I am saying is that the relationship between the two is one element, an important one, contributing to the well-being prevailing within the planet. Nor, as the reader is by now aware, would I neglect the psychological pole (if I may use a favored term of Whitehead's) contributing to this well-being. Most especially is this present in humans; we have the greatest capacity for appreciating the peace that can prevail between ourselves and other living things, the harmony that care yields. But I believe this capacity (again following Whitehead) is present as well in all living things — though I admit with growing diminishment the farther away we move from ourselves on the evolutionary line. The insect on the rose outside my window can feel peaceful rest, harmony with its surrounding world, as can my cats, as can I. If this sounds peculiar, or even ridiculous, it is because you and I do not share the same vision of the Earth and its life, and I have not yet been able to convince you of the legitimacy of mine.

With regard to ourselves as one of the societies on Earth, the human society, it seems to me a truism that there can be no peace among us, and thus no lasting health, until there is peace within us. And it seems equally as true that there can be no peace within us until we accept the fact that the Earth is not ours alone but is shared with all its other inhabitants — that if we enjoy any prerogative toward non-human life it is that of a shepherd, a good shepherd as this goodness is partly described in Jesus' famous parable. Only with the abandonment of our conceit toward other forms of life (particularly, in my view, other animal life) can we strengthen the humility needed to recognize that as only one species on this planet we cannot "go it alone" to achieve the healing therapy of the peace we desire. For peace, after all, is not merely the absence of a killing hostility between us. It is also the result of the felt presence, and with it a corresponding veneration, of the beauty, wonder, and privileges of the life, the other societies mated with us in the body of the Earth.

A delicate issue has again emerged, and it must now be addressed directly. Throughout these pages I have written of certain rights and privileges as if these belonged to animals in and of themselves. I have done so because I believe this. Yet I recognize that others may not. To these I would say that if you cannot share my own belief, at least recognize your power to *bestow* these rights and privileges — that their absence represents a choice of your will. In Genesis this bestowing power was affirmed when Yahweh gave Adam the right to name the animals; in the Old Testament thought this mythology illustrates, to name something is to grant it certain prerogatives. We have already seen that one of these was the right of animals not to be used as food sources (though this was later superseded by the covenant with Noah). What authority we possess over other lives must be exercised with the greatest discretion, seeking to honor this life and affirm its innate worth. For "authority" derives from the verb *authoritein*, meaning to set free; it implies a refusal to intrude on the life of another in any except liberating ways.

The above remarks require what Gabriel Marcel (I think it was he) called an "expansivity" in the horizons of our thought. We must learn to extend the values we profess, such as respect for life, to ever-increasing applications. This demands discipline on our part, often the unhappy abandonment of old patterns of thought for the sake of new ones we are convinced represent a better, more sensitive or effective approach to our experiences and the behavior they shape. However, to admit this power we have to change our attitudes or values — many of which may have been with us a very long time, feeling comfortable and secure like a favored armchair before an open fire — does not mean we have the inclination. It is the inclinations we have, then, about the power we possess that need our thoughtful attention. Before we can reverence animals, for example, we must first learn to become inclined (meaning to lean or tend, to be favorably disposed) toward this reverence. Without this inclination, our reverence remains merely an abstraction, a pleasant word with no action justifying its use. This is the same inclination also needed before faith in God can become effective. Many religions assert that God is anthropotropic, meaning that God does not ignore but is always leaning toward humanity, much like heliotropic plants always lean toward a source of light for nourishment and growth. What religious faith requires is that we become theotropic, God-leaning, if this faith is to be nourished and grow in vibrant, influential ways.

My use of the word "reverence" brings me finally to another theological consideration. The Old Testament prophet Micah tells us that there are only three things the Lord asks of us: do the deeds of justice, practice loving kindness, and walk humbly with your God. I would like to suggest that these represent a hierarchy and, further, that there are no restrictions on them. If so, then the deeds of justice we do must involve not just our human relationships, but those with all living things. A fairness is required in how we treat them, an awareness of their dignity and worth beyond the scope of their usefulness to us. The same may be said of loving kindness. We learn from Jesus more than Micah that this loving kindness must have the characteristics of *agape*. It must include more than what we find lovable, our family, friends, and so on. It must be indiscriminate in its expression toward all life, not asking for appreciation or rewards, not needing praise or the recognition of others. It is this loving kindness we show when we respond helpfully to an animal in need or protect one being abused, or simply share our days in caring ways with an animal grown dependent on us.

There is a venerable idea in the history of religious thought that states that the Earth (in some versions, the whole universe) is God's body. One purpose of the idea is to teach us that all creation is sacred, and that to misuse or demean any portion of it is therefore a sacrilege. We saw something similar to this sanctification of all things in chapter two, when noting the equally venerable idea that everything participates in the spirit of divine being. When Micah tells us that we are required to walk humbly with our God, one meaning his injunction might then possess is that we are to treat the Earth and all its dwellers not just as a living organism but as the living God. The humility described a few paragraphs back thus takes on a more profound meaning than simply the acknowledgment that we need help meeting the tasks of our existence. Now it recognizes that this help must be divine, but that access to it comes only through the world around us, all its occupants who form the societies giving life and health to God's body.

Finally, while images like the above may repel some people, for others they ground an exquisite and sensitive spirituality. As I said before, it is not the images that matter but the thought underlying them. If we see as one of our tasks in life the care of animals, and if we see these animals as participants in the very life and well-being of God, then the spirituality suffusing our behavior, marked by a humility confessing our limits, will indeed be both exquisite and sensitive. But there is no new access here to holiness. For the holiness is all around us, only waiting to be invited into our lives, treated as we would treat any honored guest greater and wiser than we, with deference and a willingness to learn.

CHAPTER FIVE

❧

Killing Seasons

❧

When I was a young man, a friend of mine, a tropical fish enthusiast, had purchased two male Bettas (also known as Siamese fighting fish), which he was eager to show me. Separated by a glass wall in the aquarium, their mutual but ineffective aggression toward each other lent the color in their fins an almost luminescent beauty. I was content with the passing moments watching them, until my friend asked if I knew anything about this particular species of fish. Being a beginning novice in the field, I said no. In response he removed the partition separating them, and my contentment quickly changed to horror. There before my eyes the two males tore at each other, biting off large pieces of fin, one even plucking out the eye of the other. The hostility lasted about twenty minutes, until one of the fish was dead. The other died the next day.

I have noted repeatedly throughout these pages examples of human brutality toward animals. Now we have an instance of animals brutalizing each other — and even more, for no apparent reason. Both fish had sufficient personal territory (the body of the mature male Betta measures about two inches; the tank they were in held fifteen gallons). They were bountifully fed by their owner. There was no female present to provide immediate mating competition. Neither fish was ill or indicated behavioral abnormalities. Their hostility, in short, appeared innate, as if it were built into them by the frequent perversity of game-playing genes. For all the world it seems that male Bettas are "programmed" to expend their efforts killing each other. I sometimes wonder if humans are much different. Watching those two fish doing their murderous dance with each other, or studying the tale of human history, can produce a paralyzing fear, a stillborn hope about the goodness of life.

There is a certain ideology of survival that prevails among animals. It is often individually oriented: the one animal does whatever it can to stay alive. But the ideology can also encompass a whole group, usually members of the same species, so that individuals within this group, sometimes large numbers of them, will die to ensure the survival of the remaining members. This phenomenon is known to everyone. It provides one rationale for the protectiveness we find among animals, what some biologists call the altruism in animal behavior. But it provides no rationale for the violence of our two male Bettas. It too is lacking from the foregoing list of motives that might make sense of their actions, so that our judgment about the apparent innateness of their mutual hatred still seems valid. To be sure, we might theorize imaginatively about their behavior. Perhaps the way they wiggle their fins or roll their eyes or position their mouths is analogous to similar provocative gestures human beings make toward each other. But we have no convincing evidence that this is the case.

I use the word "ideology" above advisedly. An ideology

is usually understood as the product of reflective consciousness — a system of thought, prejudiced in a particular direction and tenaciously defended, that shapes values and consequently behavior. I certainly would not argue that non-human animals possess reflective consciousness. There is no evidence as yet that they do, especially among such creatures as oysters and dragonflies (among the higher classes of mammals, however, we must have care in our assessment; our descriptions of what constitutes reflective consciousness are biased toward a defense of its human manifestations as the standard of judgment). Yet if we prune this element of reflective consciousness from our definition and speak of any behavior dominated by certain goals and diligently pursued as an ideology, then I think we can fairly speak of an ideology of survival among all animals. More than that, I think we can also speak of an ideology of violence among them.

Our male Bettas are good examples of this ideology of violence. So too is the black widow spider, though in her case we could argue that the reason she kills and consumes her mate after fertilization is to nourish herself while gestating the eggs holding her young. The mate dies as one way to help insure the survival of the many. Then there is the example of the praying mantis. I have been told that this is the one animal, in addition to human beings, that apparently kills simply for the "sport" of it, not as a response to a threat, not to protect territory, not even necessarily to nourish itself. The female not only typically kills her mate after fertilization, sometimes but not always consuming parts of him, she (and he while still alive) will also indiscriminately kill any other insect within striking range of her prodigious mandibles, leaving whole populations of carcasses in her wake. But if the behavior of this insect shocks you, I can also tell you of a poll taken some time ago among children thirteen years old. They were asked what they would most enjoy doing on Halloween. The majority of them said they would like to kill someone. When asked why, they simply said, "to see what it is like" or "for the fun of it."

Most of us enjoy the sight of a well-kept flower garden. The beauty produces serenity, and the serenity relaxes us. But this is from a distant view. For if you look closely at what goes on in a garden, serenity dissolves into aversion, because what you see is no longer attractive but loathsome. On this closer view the garden is no longer a place of beauty but of awesome violence, like a madhouse where sociopaths have broken free. You see insects not only attacking and shredding the plants as food sources but also each other. You see ants herding aphids up a plant stalk then biting off the aphids' wings so they can't escape. You see our friend the praying mantis wholeheartedly beheading anything her own size or smaller, like the Queen of Hearts in Alice's wonderland lopping off the heads of her own kind on a mere whim. The garden has become a panorama of mutual brutality among animals, and instead of a place of life it comes increasingly to look like a morgue. The aggression in human spirits that Sigmund Freud, Konrad Lorenz, Erich Fromm, and others have analyzed is indeed matched in the behavior of many non-human animals, like the mindless killing play of demented children. The difference, though, is that none of these other animals, only human beings, has that singular possession that Jeremiah says is more important as a guide to behavior than anything else — a conscience capable of knowing good from evil, written on our hearts, the prophet says, by God.

A biologist friend of mine once told me that if it weren't for human beings this period in which we live would be called the Age of Insects, that these tiny animals would be the dominating life form on the planet. I have no cause to doubt him. All of us know about the seemingly inexhaustible energy of insects, the strength of many out of all proportion to their size, their adaptability to changing ecosystems, their ferociousness toward each other (or when grouped together, like swarms of bees or ants, toward animals much larger than them), their clever ways of camouflage, their diligence and often speed in fleeing an enemy, and so on. The survivability of insects is uncanny, their resort to offensive or defensive violence unnerving. Even with all the chemicals we have directed against them, the sprays and pellets and powders, even with the most sophisticated traps, the introduction of ravenous insectivores, the swatting and pinching and foot stomping we do to kill them, the insects are still far and away the most successful class of animals on Earth, if success is measured in numbers and persistence through time.

Yet when you look closely at a garden, this success is merely an abstraction from the life individual insects enjoy. It is a life of constant alertness, fright, and little rest, one almost entirely devoid of trust, a suspicious life that presumes every other insect, let alone other animals, is on a hunt. I am not dissuaded from using such vocabulary, words like "trust" and "suspicion," which we usually reserve only for human behavior. I will not distill what I see in the sterile and overly precise jargon of biology textbooks, nor descend to the use of a language that speaks of living things as one might speak of plastic. To be sure, there is beauty in the life of animals, enchantment that captures our minds. But there is also rampage, the ruthless savagery of a killing season that never ends. We human beings are taught that Armageddon will occur only once, at the end of our history. But every day brings Armageddon to these small creatures, with no certainty that they will end the day's battles victorious and alive.

We can make similar observations about other, larger animals as well. I once saw a film of a lioness stalking an antelope. The antelope was at a watering hole among the grasses of an open savannah, its eyes and ears constantly surveying the immediate terrain for the presence of any predators. But the lioness stalked very carefully, hidden from view and unknown to her prey. Then, about sixty feet away, she leaped. The antelope spotted her and started running at a zigzagging pace clearly faster than the lioness could run. But it was an open savannah, and it was clear that while the antelope was initially quicker and more agile than the cat, it was simply a matter of time before the lioness's greater stamina would win the race. Long before exhaustion, therefore, the antelope just stopped and turned toward the lioness, the camera capturing not so much fear now as resignation in the animal's eyes. The lioness struck, and with two bites at the throat the antelope was dead. All of us have seen such films. Some will admire the stealthiness of the cat, her diligence and care in the hunt. Others, like myself, remember above all else the fear, then resignation, in the antelope's eyes, greeting unexpected and unwanted death in paralytic silence. The eyes finally close, with blood gushing from the neck, and there is no more life.

I suspect that most of us who think more of the antelope than the lioness do so because we identify ourselves more as prey than as predators. I will be very blunt. I believe that we live in a largely perverse and paranoid culture. We would never agree with the famous sentiment expressed by Blanche in Tennessee Williams's remarkable play, *A Streetcar Named Desire*, "I have always relied on the kindness of strangers." It is the word "always" that prohibits our agreement. Strangers can be kind, yes; but our media, perhaps our own experiences, tell us that often they are not. They can be just as cunning and careful, just as killing as a lioness stalking an antelope. Admittedly, I have also seen films where a lioness walks in full view and close proximity to a herd of antelopes; the antelopes sense that at the moment there is no danger, no need to flee. I have had similar confidence walking among large groups of people. But when I am alone walking my neighborhood, especially at night, a camera would record on my face continual alertness, dappled with fear, to any unexpected movement nearby.

In a previous chapter I quoted a line from Tennyson's magnificent poem, *In Memoriam*. I would now like to quote it again within the stanza in which it appears:

Who trusted God was love indeed
And love Creation's final law —

Though Nature, red in tooth and claw
With ravine, shrieked against his creed—

This stanza, in fact the whole poem, has been subject to many interpretations. But one thing at least is clear, a painful dichotomy, a split between God's will and what we find in the natural world around us. If God's will for created life is centered on love, Nature's seems centered on a bloodletting swing between chase and flight. It is this discrepancy that theologians call the sin of the world. It should not be ignored or dismissed with a flippant remark, nor even mourned with unproductive feelings. What is called for are deeds contributing to the atonement of this sin, loving, shaping, redemptive deeds. And of all the animals the task of doing such deeds is ours alone, if we claim, as many do, that we are God's very image on Earth.

∽

I spoke a few pages back of what some biologists describe as altruism in animal behavior. An often cited illustration is the single bird, spotting a predator, who cries to warn others in the vicinity, thereby drawing the predator's attention to itself. Another would be the baboon who fights a clearly stronger or more lethally equipped marauder so that the rest of the pack has time to seek safety. Still another would be the phenomenon of the feral mother, the female animal who will die before letting harm come to her babies. Since I have already noted my belief in the legitimacy of applying affective terms to such behavior, I too have no difficulty in calling it altruistic. Knowing of such actions, perhaps lucky enough to have seen them, softens somewhat the spectacle of self-interest or indifferent brutality described in previous paragraphs. We grow more comfortable in assigning goodness to some activities of animals.

Not everyone, of course, would agree with the tone of the above analysis, including, I suspect, most biologists. They might prefer to say, for example, that the so-called altruism of animals is actually the result of a coded genetic response, wrapped up in the mysteries of DNA, to species, not individual or even small group, survival. The issue here is still debated, sometimes with considerable temper, among those trained in the life sciences, more so by those in bioethics. I myself have always found it somewhat unsettling to think that concern for species survival dominates universally *and* blindly over the defense responses, and so the survival, of individual animals. One of the results this idea requires, along with the refusal to acknowledge altruism in animal behavior, is that we truncate the Judeo-Christian (though not always the Buddhist) viewpoint that the individual within any given community has certain privileges precisely as a member of that community, that one of these is the worth of the individual's life, and that this is extended (at least by Jesus) to all living things, including the single failing sparrow of whom God is aware. And it brings to mind another stanza from *In Memoriam:*

> Are God and Nature then at strife
> That Nature lends such evil dreams?
> So careful of the type she seems,
> So careless of the single life.

My unsettled mind, however, leads me to reflection not just on a stanza from a poem; it also leads me to remembrance of something I once saw. It was a warm July evening and I was visiting a friend. About four weeks earlier her cairn terrier had delivered a litter of puppies, of which four were still alive. Like most people, I found the puppies irresistible, and was sitting on the floor playing with them while my friend left the room. When she returned she was holding in her hands a kitten of indecipherable parentage, perhaps three weeks old. She told me to watch closely what would happen next. As my friend put the kitten on the floor, I did indeed watch as the kitten made his way toward the mother terrier, who was lying down about eight feet away. To my enormous delight, when he reached her she started licking the top of his head while he suckled and began drinking her milk. The puppies quickly spotted this, scurried to their mother, and also began to nourish themselves. It was a sight I had never witnessed before, though I had heard of such things happening.

To what possible species concern was the terrier responding? None of which I know. The kitten was not only of a different species, but of a different genus and family. Yet there was the terrier cleansing and nursing him. It gave me a clear and unqualified reason for modifying my allegiance to the idea that animals always behave according to an ideology of survival, let alone an ideology of violence. Caring for that kitten served not at all the terrier's concern for species endurance, nor did she see the kitten as a present or potential threat to herself or her puppies. All she did was to behave altruistically, giving of herself to an animal otherwise bereft of the pleasures of being intimately washed and fed. The terrier made the kitten feel accepted, secure, content in a world he did not yet know was also threatening and malevolent.

We also see this altruism taking a more oblique form in the fidelity demonstrated by animals toward each other, a type of loyalty and commitment not to the group or species but to one other individual. Doves are perhaps the most widely known illustration of this, two companions mated for life, each attentive to the needs of the other, sharing food and mutual preening, always alert and ready to warn the partner of the near presence of a predator. Two such doves live in a scrubby woods across the street from me. I have been seeing them off and on for years, and each time I do I envy their devotion, sensing that should one die, the other would be quick to follow, as sometimes happens in human relationships. It is difficult to analyze, but easy to appreciate, the profound attachment of two lives when this mutual death occurs.

I am condemned to be a theologian, a Christian one at that. I tend to look everywhere for affirmations or denials of the teachings of Jesus, and I use these teachings (insofar as I understand them) as the fundamental basis for my assessment of behavior. And just as I believe that one day all living things, not just human beings, will be raised from the dead, so I believe that many of the teachings of Jesus as the basis for assessing behavior apply across the board, not just to what human beings do. When I see a mother terrier nursing an abandoned kitten, therefore, I see the canine equivalent of the injunction of Jesus, stated in a variety of ways throughout the gospels, that we must give all we have to the aid of the poor. If you find this judgment offensive, sacrilegious, or silly in its viewpoint, so be it. But I remain convinced of its appropriateness. And fidelity to convictions, yours or mine, is not just a catalyst for reasoned and well-argued dialogue; it is also the parent of honor, the honor, at its purest, of a man crucified on Golgotha.

Despite such examples of altruism in animal behavior, however, we cannot lose sight of the violence we also discover. And not just violence, but the selfishness we discover as well. A parasite, for example, is an animal that feeds itself on the body of another animal, its so-called host. No serious damage is usually done to the host, unless the parasite becomes pernicious, its colonies too large or too active for the host to maintain. Some types of worms in dogs and cats and other animals too, including human beings, are parasites. As we just said, they are usually not hostile; they are just selfish, taking what they need for their own sustenance but giving nothing in return. In fact, on a wider application we might even describe our lioness as a parasite on the antelopes she hunts; she takes what she needs but gives nothing, save death, no contribution at all, to her prey (the idea that she is eliminating weaker members from the antelopes' gene pool, and thus serving the herd as a whole, is only sometimes true; frequently she catches a robust antelope who, surprised or not, just doesn't have the speed, agility, or stamina she does). And some human beings, too, are parasites, spiritually or psychologically now, not physically. We also are animals quite capable of taking from others and giving nothing in return.

The counterpart to parasitism is symbiosis, a relationship of mutual advantage between animals. The remora is a fish that suctions itself on the body of a shark, typically around the mouth and forward gills. The relationship is accepted by both animals because while the remora has security and a food source (the bits and pieces of prey that escape its companion's gnashing jaws) clinging to the shark's body, the shark is also served because the remora rids its skin of bothersome, potentially dangerous, parasites. A similar relationship also exists between ourselves and certain types of bacteria within our bodies. We provide them with nutrients in our tissues and blood to feed on, while they, for example, assist our digestive process. Symbiosis benefits not just one or the other partner, but both. Both take as well as give what aids the health and well-being of each.

If we cannot practice an open altruism toward the animal life around us, caring but expecting nothing in return, let us at least enter into symbiotic relationships with these animals whenever we can. And if there are some whom we judge can give us nothing, and so we wish no positive relationship with them, let us just leave them alone. We should not allow this refusal or inability to form a positive relationship to justify a negative one, marked by an aggressive hostility that passively or actively approves of their damage or death (I am obviously not speaking here of animals openly antagonistic toward our health, against whom we have the right to defend ourselves). When I was a lad and a mosquito landed on me, I quickly smashed it out of existence with my hand. I did so because I had been taught that this was the proper response to a mosquito's life. Now I use a repellant to prevent the landing in the first place, or should one occur, I simply yet carefully brush the insect off me. It is not much of an effort, not much of a contribution to respect for other life forms. But it is something better than mere killing.

∽

When we look at the panorama of life in our world, we do indeed find instances of altruism. I've no doubt about this. But for the most part we do not; we see again the pain and savagery that laces itself throughout existence, like a bad dream that just won't stop repeating itself. And again the question emerges, what is the purpose of all this pain, to what end does it lead, what goal or aim? Human reflection has been engaging this question one generation following another, throughout the whole world, in every time and culture. Wrestling with it is the birthright of every child born of woman, and suggestive responses have been many. Let us take a little time to look at some of them.

One of these suggestions is that the savagery we see is the partner of the evolutionary process. The struggle for existence, we are told, is double-edged: it involves not just the struggle of life to achieve increasing levels of complexity, reaching its current apogee in human beings, but struggle among all the contributors to this end. In the course of this struggle far more species have become extinct than still survive, and the lives of most of the survivors are directed no longer by the possibility of further progress in complexity but by the simple concerns of continued existence: killing each other for food, to alleviate threat, to establish territory, to assure successful reproduction. Acceptance of this state of affairs is not a choice. It is the only option available to the intelligent mind, so that the ceaseless pain and death we see among animals, while in bittersweet moments we might mourn it, is a brute given that cannot be denied, with little being done (or able to be done) to alleviate it.

I don't like doing so, but I have to agree with the general assessment of the above response. Where I would demur is over the extent of our intervention in prohibiting the damage and slaughter of animals by each other. If little can currently be done, more can be done than is actually occurring. Better, safer shelters could be provided, reserves that could be closely policed. More food, too, could be provided, since it is well-known that enough food is grown on this planet to feed all its human inhabitants with a considerable excess left over. It is the greed, often spitefulness of corporations and nation states that prevents this, preferring to allow stored food sources, grains and the like, to rot and decay before sharing them. The evolutionary process is not impermeable; we can intrude upon it for the benefit of many living things, if we only had the desire and structured the organizations to do so. To be sure, some efforts have been made in this direction. I would cite for special praise the Chipengaali animal preserve in Zimbabwe. But much more could still be done, without deprivation to human needs.

A second suggestion (actually only a tighter specification of the first) has recently been put forward by proponents of the so-called Anthropic Principle. In one reading of this principle we are told that everything that has evolved on Earth has as its central purpose the final emergence of human life. More, this is true not just of the Earth but of the evolution of the entire universe, though not, some of these theorists concede, of alternate universes, should such things exist. To support their claim the proponents serve us amazing platters of data — the oxygen content of the atmosphere (a few percentage points one way or the other would prevent the sustenance of human life); the orbit around the sun (not too close yet not too far); the evolutionary process itself (the discretion of the selection process that chose only certain possibilities among countless others); the current failure (due to, say the "hard" proponents, the impossibility) of detecting intelligent life forms elsewhere in the observable universe; and so on and on.

In previous chapters, differing contexts, I have already indicated what my response is to ideological stances like the

Anthropic Principle. Most, perhaps all the data presented cannot be denied, or at least (as in communications from extraterrestrial intelligences) proven false. It is the interpretation of the data that bothers me, the species-centricity of it all, the ethics and aesthetics it implies. It is like a distasteful gesture to the rest of creation to say it all exists solely to produce us. Or like the bits and pieces of marble a sculptor thoughtlessly tosses aside while producing his finest work of art, it is saying that all the pain and suffering of other life-forms are mere waste-products (or in my judgment worse, necessary components) in the process leading to the evolution of human beings. This is too much, too arrogant, the nasty result of any reductionism untempered by the entertainment of other options of interpretation. It puts me in mind of debates over the nature of God, such as those between deists and theists, whose major result is a hardening of propositional beliefs into mere dogmatism.

A third suggestion is that the Earth is a limited resource and that the empty pain and dying we witness among all forms of life is actually a mechanism of population control. There is certainly some legitimacy in this viewpoint. Where I would depart from it is when it attempts to include human intervention in the control of animal populations, as if this intervention, so to speak, were doing the Earth a favor. This is ridiculous, the type of thinking, if they were sophisticated enough, our pack of good old boys from the last chapter, swilling beer and bragging about their bloodsport in killing jackrabbits, might entertain. The populations of the Earth managed their own control for countless millennia before humans appeared on the scene, and still do. In fact, if there is any species of animal whose population until now has threatened the bounty of the planet, breeding with little discretion, no natural enemies, save itself, for whom it is continual prey, consuming all it desires of what the planet offers with limited foresight on future needs, it is our own. It is as if the only command in the entire

Bible that humanity has taken seriously is, "Be fruitful and multiply."

A fourth suggestion, the one Tennyson's *In Memoriam* here and there represents, describes the savaging of life we see around us as simply the result of the indifferent, chance-ridden perversity of Nature. Everywhere we look we see Nature red in tooth and claw, and there appears no rhyme or reason to any of it, only a kaleidoscopic randomness that offends our desire for intelligent causes to events. Death as a mechanism for population control, suggested above, is of itself no longer the point. The point, rather, and we have engaged it before, is the *excessiveness* of this death, beyond the needs of population control, even to the extent of the extinction of entire species. It is as if Satan was orchestrating the fate of living things, and not just non-human life but our own as well. Among human beings too, we see unaccountable pain and dying, viruses feeding on our bodies, bacteria doing the same, cells that suddenly go wild with malignancy in their train. And then there is the irrationality of our mutual bloodletting in family, neighborhood, and national warfare. The counsel is to bow and accept these facts, sure that no effort can alter them except in minute, ultimately insignificant ways. For it is the destiny of all living things to participate in a drama whose producer and director is mindlessly evil, killing for no purpose other than the sport of it.

I am not unsympathetic to the above viewpoint and the counsel it advises. But my sympathy does not extend to a willingness to give up, sadly to accept killing seasons that never end and are too extreme, too senseless in their proportion. As I said pages ago, this would be too easy, an escape-artist's motive when refusing a feat taking more effort than he or she wants to give it. We can intrude, we must intrude to change the climate of these seasons. And if they are playing out a drama of passing earthly time, we must seek to change the script. The producer and director of the drama may not be subject to our will, our commands, but perhaps to our persuasion, the efforts we make to improve the drama, giving it increasing times of peace in place of murderous discord. To the responsive mind, now religiously tuned, this raises again the issue of God.

The apparent absurdity of so much pain and death in the world can lead to the harsh judgment that God is evil; that by any moral standards we can generate, God does not always act according to the requirements of goodness. This does not come as a surprise to many believers (the great psychologist Carl Jung would be an example) because they assert that the only reliable access we have to knowledge about God is knowledge about ourselves — and even a minimally developed consciousness is aware that human beings are both good and evil. Somewhat modified, and encouraged by an awesome confrontation with his God, the innocent but pain-ridden Job reaches a similar viewpoint: God is God, and the divine will cannot be compelled to submit to the constraints of a moral vision. Here God may still be omnipotent but is no longer all-good. And while many might be willing to accept this conclusion (refusing the option of postulating two Gods, one good and one evil), others find it unnerving, an ambiguous presence in their spiritual life.

What this second group wants, then, is a God who is indeed all-good. And yet they still find themselves confronted with the same unaccountable pain and death in the life all around them, and their God appears incapable of doing anything to heal it. Great sympathy must be shown these people, finely honed spirits who want without ambiguity to believe that all creation, and its Creator too, is finally good. With Julian of Norwich they wish to sing as the final refrain in their judgment on life, on God, "all will be well; all will be well; all manner of thing shall be well." And perhaps in the future this refrain will ring true. But for the present, like the first group above, they are caught in the same theological beartrap of deciding whether God is omnipotent but not all-good, or all-good but not omnipotent.

An imaginative feat is needed. When we take seriously the seeming absurdity of all the pain and dying that slaps our spirits, we must try to enter the mind of God. If we do, I would say the discovery awaiting us is the idea that neither power nor goodness is pre-eminent in God's relationship with creation. This privilege belongs to freedom. It is freedom that God values beyond power and goodness, bestows on all creation, refusing interference with its expressions. It is the freedom of the virus to work its way in us that kills, just as it is our freedom that seeks to prevent this killing. It is the freedom of the planet that lets its plates move in ways bringing earthquakes, just as it is our freedom in the pursuit of knowledge that allows us to predict, flee, perhaps someday even control this movement. It is freedom that allows a man to shoot a lion for sport, freedom that allows a lion to maul a young child. We should not speak of inevitabilities or instincts here that command behavior; we should speak of the freedom that allows these inevitabilities or instincts to take their course. And all this freedom, to my way of thinking, is God-given.

I owe the above idea, once more, to my understanding of the philosophy of Alfred North Whitehead. It is a good idea, analytically productive in ways that an emphasis on God's power and goodness as motives for activity is not. This is not to say, of course, that God does not possess power and goodness; no believer would make such a claim. Nor is it to say that God does not function as a free cause of events. It is to say, rather, that God is not the only cause; there are others (like viruses and climate, DNA and hungry lions) that God may seek to persuade, but does not compel, toward the doing of divine will — in my judgment now, a good, beneficent, never evil, will, the will of a blessing, non-coercive Father. All of which means that we cannot lay the burden of killing seasons solely on God's shoulders. For we too are free, like all creation, causes that, with God's good will, can temper these seasons with care and kindness.

CHAPTER SIX

∾

Beauty in the Beast

∾

I was on a journey once that took me into the high Sierras of northern Nevada. Along the way, I stopped in a small town for some refreshments, one of those towns whose inhabitants can make you feel you have done something wrong just stopping there. At the serving bar were three young men and a young woman, chomping down hamburgers and fries as fast as they were served, clad in flannel shirts and bluejeans, the favored attire of "down home" folk everywhere. I picked up on their conversation (its volume could scarcely be ignored) to find them discussing how they had killed a timber wolf the previous day. "Shot him in the hindquarters first," said one, "then tracked him and finally got him in the head." "Don't like wolves," said another, "just don't like having them around. They're bad luck." There was unanimous agreement, some backslapping, and then general boasting about how neatly the animal had been skinned. It reminded me of those men in Montana bragging about shooting jackrabbits for sport, and I wondered, not for the first time, if I was the only one whose experiences of small towns with small-minded people were so unnervingly alike.

I stayed in the café about another twenty minutes, then left. The conversation had turned to a Catholic priest who had recently begun his duties in a nearby town, the first time, apparently, any priest had taken up permanent residence in the local area. The talk was filled with all the anti-Catholic prejudice you often find in such places, crude and pornographic, suggesting sexual perversity, power-madness, witchcraft, and so on. Yet as I drove away my mind was not on the priest, though I pitied him for the harrowing days ahead, but on the wolf, dead because of stupid, superstitious people. Not once did they speak of the wolf's beauty, his grace in movement, the fine lines and coloration of his face, the smooth, pleasing texture of his fur. They did not speak of it because they could not appreciate it. So they made the wolf ugly, a fearsome, mindless predator who brought bad luck, marauding life wherever he went — a view, any informed individual knows, that is simply not true. The wolf tends to be quite shy, killing only for food or protection, and generally indulgent in sharing his territory.

There are various forms that beauty takes. One of these is the beauty of words, the language of poetry or well-written, well-spoken prose. We noted in earlier chapters the creativity of words, the way words can produce realities or experiences within us, consolation, anger, serenity, bitterness. Beauty too is one of these experiences words can create, the beauty of a described sunset, a peaceful mind, a child's first kiss, rapture with God. Animals do not speak words, except for some, and these are only imitative repetitions of what they have been taught. But while animals do not shape words on their own, they can and do communicate with each other. And beauty often resides in this communication, the beauty of birdsongs in the waking morning of a day, the loveliness of whalesong across the deep, the rhythmic purr of a cat, the mournful howl of a wolf at midnight. All we need are ears to hear, and an attentive sympathy, to discover and cherish the beauty of these sounds.

Beauty can be found not just in what we hear but also in what we see, the beauty of physical shapes and movement. This beauty crosses the boundary between living and non-living things: our sunset, a distant mountain range, the stars in a limpid night sky, oaks and orchids that communicate nothing we can hear but are still beautiful, the human body, the splendor of a tigress, the luminescence of a hummingbird's feathers or a serpent's scales. Each of us could continue this list in countless ways. But every example would indicate that sight, like hearing, is not just a defensive (or offensive) device we have inherited from our animal forebears. They are also aesthetic devices bringing pleasure to our spirits. The sadness of being deaf or blind, therefore, is not just the result of a fear of bruising, bleeding accidents, but the continual deprivation of forms of beauty these handicaps involve (I write this sentence from the perspective of a hearing, sighted man).

A third form beauty can take is that of deeds or actions. I include in this not just the beauty of human dance, for example, the chase of the jaguar and the flight of the pelican, but, especially regarding human deeds, their ethical equivalents as well. Witnessing deeds of mercy, compassion, generosity can appear as beautiful to us as the most exquisite minuet or exuberant ballet. The beauty of an old nun caring for abandoned children on the streets of Calcutta can be a match, perhaps even surpass, the beauty of movement in the performance of our finest gymnasts, our mimes and figure skaters. So too the beauty of a man releasing fireflies his child had captured, or of an itinerant preacher who went to a cross for the love of his God. This attests to the ubiquity of beauty, the fact that we can find it everywhere, prodigal in its expressions and always ready for appreciation, study, and response. It is the counterpart to the ugliness we can also find everywhere, the balance giving wholeness to our experiences of the world.

The above remarks can be extended slightly further. The beauty we find in morally pure or good deeds has a way of slipping over as the criterion for judging other activities that, strictly speaking, have no morality to them. So we say to the dancer, "That was a good performance," or, "That was a bad performance." We are not using "good" and "bad" as ethical terms but only to indicate our assessment of the technical merits of the dance, often, if we are unqualified to judge such merits, simply our subjective response. Yet with the first saying the dancer feels pride, with the second there is shame — pride and shame being distinctly moral categories. So the dancer feels that he or she has done something not only technically but morally right, or technically and morally wrong. It is such feelings that may partially explain the sometimes extreme disturbance with which a dancer, or any artist, greets criticism in the process of improving a performance. An ethical penumbra is thought to surround this criticism.

We are all aware, of course, that there is a high degree of relativity in judgments about beauty. I would never dispute this point, so that what examples I give are drawn pre-eminently from my own personal assessments, nurtured on the study of books and conversations with friends and colleagues. When we look to the dictionary too, as presumably the source for the common understanding of a word, we find an implicit recognition of this relativity: "beauty: that quality or aggregate of qualities in a thing which gives pleasure to the senses or pleasurably exalts the mind or spirit; physical, moral, or spiritual loveliness." What this means is that while I might find Bach's music beautiful, others might find it brittle and overly precise; or while I might find a slender human body lovely, others might prefer greater weight, more Rubenesque in their tastes; or while I might find the excessive accumulation of luxuries repellent, the businesswoman on Wall Street might find it quite attractive. Beauty, the tired cliché runs, is in the eye (literally and/or figuratively) of the beholder.

But I speak of a high relativity in the above remarks, not a complete relativity. There are forms and degrees of psychopathy in human behavior (by this I mean any seriously aberrant activity according to our professed ideals, as individuals or groups) that, despite the psychopath's protests, can be tolerated neither ethically nor aesthetically. There are boundaries, in other words, beyond which beauty becomes ugliness. There are lovely ornaments, for example, with which human beings have always adorned their bodies, and which can enhance the attraction of the body itself: flowers and polished stones, exquisitely woven cloth. But when a man decides to ornament the forehead of his infant son by carving a swastika on it with a knife, there is no beauty here but only degenerate illness. Or when a woman consistently deprives herself of adequate nutrition because of the cult of thinness in our society, she is not so much becoming beautiful as pathetic. Or again, when foxes are slaughtered solely to make coats draping human frames, human attractiveness is not enhanced but, in my judgment, demeaned. For this robs the beauty of its living setting and tries to rearrange it in a dead one.

As I said, there are degrees of psychopathy. While I might find a woman taking pride in her fox coat or a man in his alligator shoes not only unattractive but quite reprehensible, I would certainly put neither on a par with the father who disfigures his infant's forehead. Moreover, there are not only degrees of psychopathy but active *and* passive forms of it. The passive form takes the shape of acquiescence to behavior of which we do not approve but about which we do nothing. We do nothing because we are too indolent, or because we fear the loss of friends differing from our viewpoint, or because we believe that the disapproved behavior is so widespread, or so protected by the power of corporations or governments, that any effort we made would make no difference. And so we rue the beauty taken from us when the Earth is gouged by open-pit mining, forests denuded by clear-cutting, animal populations despoiled for reasons of luxury or superstition. But our ruefulness remains sterile. We are sad, perhaps depressed, even furious, but we do not act — and so I echo again a major refrain of this book.

Or perhaps we do not act because we have become overly familiar with the beauty surrounding our lives. I once knew a man who bred Persian cats as a serious hobby. He exhibited them at shows all over the country and had countless ribbons to prove his success in competition. His breeding stock included eight mature females and two males, with a varying number of kittens depending on the time of year. When I visited him one August, he brought me to the kittens bred so far, thirteen in all, each of which, save one, was behaving with typical kitten friskiness. I went to the one who wasn't and asked the man what the problem was. He said the kitten had a bad infection and was clearly dying. I asked what he was doing about it, and he said nothing was being done: he had enough healthy kittens, the hobby was already quite expensive, and he saw no reason to spend money on veterinary care and medication for just one sick kitten. I picked the animal up. She was stunning in her beauty, and when I asked the man if I might have her, he agreed. But it was too late, much too late to save this small part of living loveliness in our world. The veterinarian did what he could; the kitten died three days later.

I thought about the man's behavior for quite some time. He clearly cherished his cats, reveled in their beauty, and proudly displayed them to any visitor. Yet toward the one sick kitten he was dismissingly indifferent, judging her illness as simply a piece of bad luck for him that he would not attempt to alleviate. In his response this man not only proved the rightness of the saying that familiarity breeds contempt; he also demonstrated that he had learned nothing from the parable of the Good Shepherd. Beauty was like a commodity to him, almost like something he ate. When he had his fill, it didn't matter to him what happened to the remainder. If somebody else wanted it, fine; if not, it could be easily enough ignored, eventually discarded. Sated by healthy beauty, dying beauty was worth no effort to save.

∽

Beauty gives birth to love. It is because we find something beautiful, a pleasure or delight in our lives, that we begin to shape affection and attachment toward it, wishing to spend increasing amounts of time with it and arranging our routines to do so. If music is our love, we are not content with fleeting or irregular acquaintance with it; we want to make music a steady, reliable companion to us, or, as with Mozart, breath, food, and drink to us. If another human being is our love, the same desire holds. Even with God, the same is true. Love of God, like love of music or another human being, compels us toward organizing our lives so that devotion grows, study of the beloved object too, and thus the time spent wrapped in the contours of this love. So it is with love of animals, or any love at all. We posit no limits to the beauty that gives birth to love and no limits to the love itself.

We cannot, then, love what is ugly (by which I mean what we find repellent, for whatever reason, in an object) — though we must be very careful here. Nothing, after all, is *completely* lovable, perhaps not even God, if the history of human complaints against God has any merit. Yet in everything, I would say, we can find beauty, some beauty that is lovable even if very scant and insufficient to pass positive judgment on the beauty of the object as a whole. A spider might strike us on the whole as quite ugly, but we might still find beauty in the facets of its eyes, less directly, in the intricate delicacy of its web. The same might be said of the homely manatee, until we see the grace with which it swims and its gentleness in human presence, or of the ungainly giraffe until it runs, or of the simple finch until it sings. Some beauty is spectacular; the whole creature seems to radiate it, like the male peacock in full courting display. But the beauty of other creatures is minute or at first unseen, missed by the roving but unexamining eye or mind, and must be discovered.

The above comments bring us back to remarks previously made about ideals. An ideal, I said, was anything beautiful whose beauty motivated our behavior in its pursuit — not a beauty passively admired, then, but one actively engaged that we wish to make increasingly our own. But here precisely is the catch, in that we can never make it our own *entirely;* we cannot achieve or possess the ideal the way we might a piece of merchandise. And this makes the pursuit of ideals particularly difficult in our achievement-oriented culture, where possession alone is gratification and pursuit something to be gotten through as quickly as we can. But with ideals the pursuit never ends and full possession is never gained. There is always more to be had ahead of us, and gratification (with some ideals we might say blessing) can only reside in our striving for, not our possession of, the beauty ever before us. The striving ends only with death's peace.

To some the above analysis might bring to mind from Greek mythology the hapless image of old Tantalus. Because of a sin committed, he is condemned to stand in a pool of water, with luscious grapes hanging just above his head. But every time he reaches down to slake his thirst, the water recedes just beyond reach. And every time he reaches up to satisfy his hunger, the grapes withdraw in a similar way. His striving remains eternally unsatisfied. Yet while this image might appeal, it does not, in fact, accurately capture the meaning of pursuing ideals. For Tantalus gains nothing by all his effort, except perhaps the pity of onlookers. But the one who pursues ideals gains beauty in the process, its intimate satisfactions and pleasurable effects. It is just that one can never gain *all* the beauty, and so will never be fully satisfied or completely pleased. But this is what makes beauty an ideal and not, as our advertising media tirelessly insists, a commodity.

It is also what gives beauty a greatness, a strength and power over our lives that we cannot altogether tame.

Therefore, no matter how thoroughly you might pursue music's ideal beauty, there will always be further notes to chase, rhythmic patterns and silences. No matter how intimate you become in knowledge and responsiveness to another beloved human being, further knowledge still awaits and more adept responsiveness too. No matter how beautiful you find the practice of mercy, making it more and more the practice of your life, there will still remain traces of spite in your spirit, even if you're the only one who knows of them. So again with generosity or humility; lurking in the shadows of your pursuit of them, perhaps seen only by you, will be the winking eyes of greed and pride. If because of this we are each tempted to give up our striving, and we saw earlier how seductive this temptation can be, then what we need is grace. But not grace as the invisible something that popular piety says inhabits our souls when we behave well — rather, grace as strength, and with it the opportunities to engage our ideals with robust commitment.

The reflections in the last several paragraphs can be applied in any spirituality of animal care. The beauty in an animal can be obvious, like our courting male peacock or the manta ray in still, clear waters. But the beauty can be less evident, even hidden, like the spider's faceted eyes or the circus of colors inside an abalone's shell. But to whatever degree, however manifest, there is always beauty in animals, in every animal. In this it is like the spirit of God, which old dogmas and their poets, priests, and professors teach us is present everywhere in various ways. And if this beauty grows into an ideal, now affecting our behavior, we will strive as best we can, knowing we will never fully succeed, to protect it, studying and embracing it as a part of our own lives, our definition of what we ourselves are. Otherwise the beauty is still there, but it remains abstract, the life in which it dwells unbridged to our own, a passing fancy whose delight brings us no passion.

When you enter a home where the spouses have brought their marriage to a high pitch of goodness — or we might say, sanctity — one thing becomes obvious very soon. You become aware that the spouses are treating you no differently from how they are treating each other. You feel not so much like a guest, let alone a stranger, as like a third partner in the marriage. From the beginning of the marriage, when they loved only each other, they have come very close to marriage's finest ideal: the consciousness that their mutual love must be shared in their love of everyone. It is the same with the saint who loves God, not hoarding this love like a precious commodity, but sharing it abundantly and without reserve. A privatized marriage, like a privatized relationship with God, might be satisfying for the individuals involved. But it is not as good as a marriage, or a faith, that has become public, whose results are available to all.

A similar development can occur in one's relationship with animals. At first you may care for only one animal, your pet, or perhaps a small group of them with whom you have formed bonds of affection. But as time passes, and if you possess a responsive spirit, you discover that the beauty you find in your favored pets is in some fashion present in all animals. And at this point you simultaneously become aware that the love you give the favorites you must therefore give to all the others; that refusing this more generous application of your love is somehow to truncate it, to make your love less expansive, and so less beautiful than it can be. Some will be satisfied with this, saying, "so be it," and their love begins to take on tinges of selfishness, limits imposed on love but not essential to it. Others refuse this satisfaction, these limits, knowing that love, like beauty, should never be constrained. It is these people I have been applauding throughout the pages of this book.

A number of years ago, in a highly controversial procedure, the heart of a baby baboon was taken from him to replace the damaged heart of an infant girl. She lived only a short while afterward. I am not going to rehearse the anger

of the arguments surrounding this event; instead, I wish only
to employ it as a symbol. The reader may recall that in a
previous chapter I noted that the word "symbol" comes from
a Greek verb meaning to unite or to bring together. What
greater symbol can there be of our communion with animals
than the sharing of hearts? For our own language, when contemplating the communion of love, often uses just this image,
a sharing of hearts, to describe both the intimacy and generosity that love brings forth. There is beauty here, Santayana
would call it an extravagant beauty, that only the barbarous
mind cannot see, the loveliness of linking humankind to animals when a non-human heart beats in the chest of an infant
girl.

∽

A friend of mine recalls something that happened to him a
number of years ago. He was walking on the street of a very
large city, one of our deformed cities, full of decay and rot
and reeking with the stench of exhaust in its air. It was a
place worse than the most savaging jungle for any animals
who lived there, lifespans usually quite short and the time
allowed spent in frightened alertness to humans and their con-
traptions. Skeletal dogs walked this city, searching for garbage
cans in which still nutritious food had been dumped, only to
be scolded and abused by humans who would not share even
their refuse with these animals. Cats were treated similarly,
and even pigeons were screamed at, kicked at, and stoned. I
saw this city my friend described as something Hieronymous
Bosch might have painted, a nightmarish place where evil was
the order of the day and the finer sides of human sentiment
ridiculed, then ignored.

During his walk he passed a group of old houses with sur-
prisingly large yards and many full-grown shrubs and trees; it
was like an oasis in a desert. On the stoop of one of them was
sitting an old man, his clothes a melange of warring colors,

with a head and beard of the thickest white hair my friend had ever seen. All around him were chipmunks, a dozen or so of them, and instead of threatening them with voice or foot or stone, the old man was feeding them, a large and serene smile giving beauty to his face. My friend went over to him and mentioned that he must indeed like chipmunks, for the food he was giving and the smile he wore. Chipmunks standing nearby scurried off at my friend's approach, and his remark wiped the smile completely from the old man's face. He said yes, he did love the chipmunks, then paused and fixed my friend's eyes with his own. I love them, he continued, because they're not like people; they never hurt you. My friend said nothing more; neither did the old man. They parted in the awkward silence that sometimes descends when strangers meet, exchange a few words, and then go their separate ways. My friend had had an experience similar to one of my own described in a previous chapter, that of an old woman feeding pigeons in a park. Both speak of the spiritual pain many elderly people suffer when the years have been unkind to them.

Some people are uncomfortable with the idea that an individual might love animals more than other human beings. But I am not; in fact, I believe it is quite understandable. We regularly find in animals the expression of virtues whose absence or unreliability in our own kind makes these animals attractive, evoking our attention to them. And it is not just their lack of intentional violence toward us, like the old man's chipmunks. In previous pages we have also spoken of their fidelity, the way they stir our humor, their guilelessness. Obviously I am not speaking of all animals here; rather, I am thinking especially of certain kinds of birds and mammals. In their company the hurt of human behavior toward us is somewhat healed, our spirits can find harbors of peace, our fears withdraw. These animals might not be inducing these effects on us intentionally; the relationship between their will and mind is still largely undetermined. But intentional or not, "virtue" is as good a word as any to describe the effect of their presence on us.

I am not ignoring in these remarks the interests of the previous chapter. Much of animal behavior does not strike us as virtuous; we find it either repugnant or frightening. But even here — in the ways animals maraud and slaughter each other — we might find oblique traces of virtue, an innocence that belies premeditation, in legal terms, malice aforethought. If I may borrow the title from one of Loren Eiseley's books of poems, animals are "innocent assassins." They do not plot or plan for the sake of murderous intentions built on spite or anger or greed the death of other animals; this is a peculiarly human prerogative. They kill, it is true, but only to feed or protect themselves, their kin group, their territory. Even the praying mantis does not ponder her savagery the way human beings do, posing options back and forth on the most lethal, blood-letting, or torture-ridden course to pursue. She simply strikes and kills, innocent of alternatives.

Nor are animals subject to the forms of insanity we are. True, there are chemical imbalances that can make an animal's behavior erratic, infections that can cause abnormal aggression and hostility. But animals do not think themselves, imagine themselves into insane acts. A lioness who kills and consumes her crippled cub is not acting insanely, no matter how repulsed we might be by what she has done. She is sparing the cub future pain, a life where survivability is far more menaced than were the cub normal, as well as nourishing herself for the better care of her remaining babies. But the sister of a student of mine who drowned her infant son while bathing him, because she claimed the image of Satan had appeared on his face, is very definitely, sadly, corruptly insane. Animals have no religion, with its attendant system of beliefs; as far as we know, none of them, save the human sort, think of deities and demons, dogmas, liturgies, sin and salvation, heaven or hell. Some would say that in this they are more blessed by God than we are.

In human art the virtues of animals, even their mutual yet innocent assassinations, are time and again portrayed. So also is the beauty of their body form, the grace of their movements. As we saw in chapter two, from Egypt there are the lovely carvings of Bast, Anubis, and Thoth, the cat, jackal, and calf deities, to which we can add exquisite renderings of crocodiles, cranes, serpents, and even beetles — the sphinx too, with its man's head and lion's body symbolizing the unity between humanity and animals. And we know the simple lines of a fish provide the emblem of early Christians, the eagle of American tenacity, the bear of Russian strength. And then there is the mother wolf suckling Romulus and Remus, the founders of Rome, and the sheep whose breath gives warmth to the infant Jesus in so many portraits of his nativity. I too have drawn dragonflies and angel fish, the faces of pumas and parrots, not great art, not even good, but an attempt to preserve the beauty I saw for future pleasure.

It seems appropriate that in this chapter on the beauty of animals I should also mention the beauty of those people devoted to their care and protection, in far more serious ways than are preserved in my drawings. I am speaking of organizations here, and the individuals participating in them, like Animal Aid, the Fund for Animals, Greenpeace, the Humane Society, People for the Ethical Treatment of Animals (PETA), and so many more. I cannot speak too highly of these organizations, the generosity of time and money their participants expend on the well-being of animals. There is, I say, beauty here, the beauty of deeds recognizing that the Earth is not home just to human beings but to all its life, bringing certain rights and privileges to each. Because we are the smartest or the most clever does not mean we are the best of the planet's creatures. But it does mean we have the greatest responsibility for our behavior.

Organizations like the above have as their primary task the care of abandoned or unprotected animals, and this almost exclusively means mammals, especially cats and dogs, though

Greenpeace emphasizes marine mammals. But if you examine the literature carefully, you also discover a concern for preserving the beauty of animals, the aesthetic comfort their mere presence gives us, as well as the way this beauty is demeaned by the enormity of human indifference to their needs or the rapacity of human greed in hunting them. I agree that there are such things as animal rights, though I also know these rights cannot be articulated by animals, successfully defended against determined human invasion. They can only be bestowed upon animals by us, as I noted earlier, the way Genesis says Adam bestowed names on all living things. But if the Genesis narrative is taken seriously, then the bestowal of names, with (from the biblical perspective) the distinct privileges a name brings with it, is not just the prerogative of human beings but the desire of God.

Names no longer have the power for us that they did for ancient peoples. We select names for things typically on the basis of their appeal to us: we like the name we have chosen. Yet we can still recognize something of the truth of the ancient ways, and we can organize ourselves so that the responsibility that our intelligence and cleverness give us extends beyond our own species concern to a reliable concern for all the living things under our care — because to name something means not only to possess authority over it but responsibility for it, a bestowed respect for its co-existence with us. To the extent, therefore, that we have so organized ourselves, as in the groups named above, I would say that we are acting not only according to the finest tenets governing the exercise of our authority and responsibility in the world, but also according to the will of God. And in both cases, too, I would say that our behavior is something beautiful, attractive to all save those for whom beauty means nothing or those who wish to constrain their definition of beauty in unnecessary and shortsighted ways.

In one tradition of Buddhism, the Mahayana, the highest point of human development, short of achieving Nirvana, is represented by the bodhisattva. And the most honorable of the bodhisattvas are those who refuse to enter Nirvana until all the suffering in the world is healed. And by this is meant human suffering, true, but the suffering of all living things as well. For while the bodhisattva believes that in some rare instances suffering can enhance living beauty, for the most part suffering diminishes, even eradicates it (the Buddhist, in other words, would find odd the idea sometimes present in old Christian pieties that suffering in itself is salvific, somehow pleasing to God and therefore something to be actively sought). Can there be a more noble ethic than this, that an individual delays the achievement of his or her religion's highest reward for the sake of assisting the healing of all life's pain? If there is, I do not know of it. Most of the ethical or moral proposals of which I am aware concern themselves with little more than the achievement of human happiness or purpose within the boundaries of human, sometimes coupled with God-oriented, relationships.

Yet the Buddhist ethic is not a completely isolated one. For we frequently do find floating throughout the history of Judeo-Christian thought the belief that a time will come when *all* will be redeemed, a new Earth born of the old where there will be no more tears or pain or death. This is the eschaton, an invitation to lyricism, the moment when God will act to bring everlasting peace, an undisturbed tranquility and harmony to the whole of creation. Unlike the bodhisattva in Buddhist teaching, then, here it is God who has become beautiful by this future deed — an object of hope for a better life beyond death that has consoled distressed human spirits since this hope was first born in them. But the consolation also soothes the worried mind's care about animals. For they too will know this new Earth, all of them with all of us. And the beauty of God's redeeming deed will refresh, enrich, and maintain the beauty of all living things, bonded in love, wedded in mutual reverence, giving thanks that the ambiguities of life, the uncertainties of even the strongest hope, have been resolved in a reality now both beautiful and good. Our present task, as it has always been and will remain until God acts, is to show ourselves worthy of this new reality.

CHAPTER SEVEN

൬

Memories That Teach

൬

Many memories have leaked from my mind onto the pages of this book. Some have given me great pleasure to recall; others have rehearsed unhappy experiences. That is the way memories work. We seldom have control over them, never complete control, and they come to consciousness one after the other like a fast-spinning carousel of good and bad. Sometimes the carousel slows or stops long enough for us to have conversations with our memories, objective conversations that are clear and precise regarding what we remember, or subjective ones in which we feel free to reshape the data and interpretation of what happened, the way a brutalizing father might reshape in later years the memory of his relationship with his children into one of benevolence. Much of the time, however, the carousel moves too quickly to give us more than rapid glimpses of the past, memories that dissolve into forgetfulness almost as soon as they emerge before our mind's eye.

Perhaps for many people it is best this way. Concentrating on the present is drain enough on their stamina; a devoted attentiveness to their past (or future) would sap them of what little mental energy they had left.

I am a man who has not been blessed with much physical vigor. It seems I am always suffering one infection or illness after another, and I need a lot of sleep. At forty years of age my heart went bad on me, developing a hankering for arhythmic tachycardia. At forty-one I was walloped with viral pneumonia, which put me out of commission for a year — this on top of a whole life history perforated with infestations of various kinds, particularly, as with the pneumonia, of viruses, which seem to have an attraction toward me of the fixating kind, clinging and relentless. But while my physical health has not been good, I have nonetheless been blessed with much mental vigor, an energetic delight in the life of the mind that has often been my only consolation when my body has given out, a love of well-worked prose and poetry and the duel of disagreeing yet courteous opinions. If I have never had the physical stamina to do the often strenuous research of a marine biologist (which I once wanted desperately to be), I have not needed it to do the research and writing of a theologian.

I would like to share with you now some further memories I have of animals, and what these animals taught me. For though I just admitted my love for good prose and poetry, my learning, after all, like everyone else's, has not been confined to these sources. I have also learned by opening my eyes to Nature, taking it in and working it over in my mind until I believe I have gained some truth, or if not truth at least some insight, into this populated world and into myself. Lessons lie everywhere around us, and it takes only the felicitous grace of a receptive spirit to absorb them, the devoted spirit to shape them into knowledge, and the responsive spirit to allow this knowledge to form behavior. But effort, of course, is required here, exertion that does not give way to the temptation to give up. And we have noted more than once just how appealing this temptation can be.

So many memories of animals are alive in me, so many lessons they taught me still vibrant. My father was a kind man, and during my early years he was involved with an animal aid organization, not deeply but conscientiously. Specifically, he would take responsibility for the care of injured wild animals, restore them to health and then set them free. Doing this gave him feelings of tranquility and, despite success in the business world, a sense of accomplishment he garnered from no other task. I remember how I would wait for him to come home in the late afternoon, to see if he had stopped at the organization's kennels and brought another animal needing care. For even at an early age the animals bewitched me as much as him and the greatest pleasure I knew was his permission to assist him in helping them. One day he came home with a horned owl whose wing was broken. The animal was frightened beyond description and, like many in this state, had become paralyzed in movement, save for some twitching above the eyes, rapid glances, and a pounding chest.

My father gave the owl a mild sedative, set the broken wing, force-fed her with a rubber syringe, and then said we should depart to allow her the calming influence of privacy. We kept all the animals under our care in a small barn-shaped building, well heated and lighted, about two hundred feet from our house, and four, five, six times a day I would go out there to check on what my mother called our "guest." After several days the owl began to bother me. She remained listless, though ate her food, and the wing did not appear to be getting sturdier. I had images of a permanent convalescence and the sadness of a seven-year-old boy who thought the owl might never fly free again. I thought she might feel about being stuck forever with a broken wing the way I felt about being stuck forever at the age of seven, never reaching thirteen, a magical age for me when I believed all kinds of wonderful things would happen, including senior status in

Little League and being quit of Catholic grammar school and its demanding regimen.

So one day I told my father of my distress. He winked at me and said the reason why the owl was taking so long to heal was to teach me patience. He told me that some physical hurts, like the hurts in our feelings, took much time before they got better, and that trying to rush the process not only didn't help but could even worsen what was wrong. It was a simple message, easy words, for a seven-year-old boy to understand. I went to bed that night much comforted and determined to wait for what could not be hastened. Eventually the owl's wing did heal and she flew free at last; tears were my only comment on her departure. But I will never forget her, the texture of her feathers, the almost purr-like sounds from within, and the guidance she gave me, partnered with my father, toward the meaning of patience and the slowly healing pace of time.

When I was fifteen, I found a dog roaming the street in front of my home. On the way to school that day I tried to coax the dog over to me, for he had about three feet of a broken leash on and was stumbling over it while he skittered around. I was afraid it might prevent him from successfully dodging a car. But he would only come to within about ten feet from me; if I tried to move any closer, he'd run off. So I went to school, and as the hours passed I could think only of the dog, coming to the somewhat inadvertent decision that if he were still around when I returned home, I would take care of him. He was, and I did, with no protest at all from my parents. After two hours of effort I managed to get close enough to him to take the leash off, put down bowls of food and water near the back porch, and jerry-rigged a bed of old rags under it. He was still very frightened, ears and tail down, low whimperings from his throat, but no external damage I could detect. I was beginning to like him very much.

During the following days the dog and I became increasingly companionable. He had been well cared for, coat groomed, a healthy weight, and, to my mother's enormous relief, housebroken. We concluded that he had broken free from his owner and wandered around until he was lost, though no one answered the various advertisements we placed for two weeks in the local newspapers and foodstores, even the church bulletin. He followed me everywhere, wanting nothing more than to lie in my lap and be petted, an unwieldy feat for a German Shepherd-plus-something-else and a fifteen-year-old boy. But we managed. And I began to realize that all this dog wanted, what he needed most, was to be loved, and in return would give his complete loyalty, not like that of the self-serving sycophant, the flatterer whom scripture scorns, but the loyalty that comes from gratitude for what someone has done for you. He would pine while I was away at school, though my mother gave him great affection, and every time he saw me after even the shortest absence, he would leap and twirl as if I had been away a lifetime. His happiness in my presence made me feel wonderful.

Until this dog entered my life, I had no experience of the need to be loved. For I had been raised in a climate of love, a place where love was the order of the day, and by me at least was taken for granted. But with the dog I began to appreciate the need, and in later years, when I left home and began to experience human relationships whose climates were hatred or spite or bitterness or despair, my appreciation grew profound. And to the advice of an old priest, that it made no difference if human beings loved you since God always did, I had no answer, though I knew he was wrong. It did make a difference, an incalculable one, to the health of human spirits to be loved by at least one other person. It is this love alone that can make our spirits twirl and jump and dance to its silent music within us the way a dog did years ago because I loved him. When he died I buried him with a kiss, and his bones, I hope, still embrace the golden rose I laid upon his chest.

Since I was nine years of age I have always kept an aquarium or two of tropical fish; right now I have three. It pleases and calms me to watch their movements, angel fish and gouramis, platies and tetras, fresh water flounders and eels, even the clownish catfish. They are so graceful, so fluid in their maneuvers and acrobatics, their seemingly effortless flow through the medium of their world. Sometimes late at night I will turn off all the lights, save those above the tanks, and listen to Mozart while I watch the fish. And the tempo of the music begins to appear so closely calibrated with their movements that I often think they hear it through the glass and water and are responding to its beauty. I know, of course, that this isn't so, but it pleasures me twice over, the way the sound and the sight blend together. I did this very thing the night of the day my dog died, to ease my fitfulness and soothe my grief, to give me something to think about other than him. It worked, a little. Even the great Mozart and the loveliness of swimming creatures can only do so much to bring serenity to a distressed human spirit.

Down the years I have watched my fish countless times. And their grace of movement has taught me about the grace of thinking we humans can achieve, when our thought is no longer brittle and unchanging, but fluid and receptive to the experiences we have. We can move through the environment of our minds, if we choose, with the same ease and adaptability these animals show when moving through their environment. We can learn to think new thoughts without feeling threatened by them, to cast off ancient but useless beliefs, hardened yet foolish prejudices in favor of more beneficial, encompassing, and caring beliefs, new thoughts whose prejudices are premised on the pursuit of what is good and giving. This gracefulness of thought, taught me by simple life swimming in a glass enclosure — we must bring it to contemplation of ourselves, our world, our God, even to how we think of such things as an owl with a broken wing and a dog who has died.

໐ᴖໆ

Sometimes events happen to us that at the moment seemed quite insignificant. It is only with later reflection, when we begin to assess the contours our life has taken, that we see the importance these events possessed. It may be true that most major turning points in life are deliberately engaged. We bring to the event, say, a marriage, as much wisdom and fore-thought as we can in order to achieve some assurance of how it will affect the course of our existence. For no one wishes to barge through life blindly and stupidly. Yet other turning points are more surreptitious in character, easing us into di-rections not against our will, but, more accurately, despite our will, until we discover what has happened and begin to look for its source. Often this results in amazement, the somewhat unsettling insight that components of what we have become, not just physically but spiritually too, have their parentage in events we first deemed unimportant. It gives us an awareness of the frailty of our control over even the best planned and tutored life we had in mind for ourselves.

It is memory, of course, that is the gateway to this aware-ness: memory as the accurate recollection of past events, coupled with illuminating judgment regarding their current meaning for us. And so I rehearse for you throughout this book, but in this chapter particularly, certain memories I have of events that I now know gave shape to what I have become as a creature composed of certain values, or better, a creature striving after certain values. And these memories, simply be-cause it is my purpose in these pages to do so, are attached to experiences of animals. Were I writing another kind of book I might emphasize my memories of other human beings, or those of my work as a gardener, or those of my lover's quar-rel with God. But in the forefront here are my memories of animals, the teachers and companions of the spirit of a quite ordinary man.

My oldest cat is named Origen, after the great theolo-gian of third-century Christianity who, unfortunately, had only faint regard for animals, seeing them, as many others did and still do, as little more than tools for human use. When he was four years old I decided to get him a companion, a female kitten who, I preferred, would be a calico. So I went to the local Humane Society to see what kittens they had in keeping. It was the first time I had ever been inside a Humane Society building, and I was very impressed. The waiting room was fairly large and comfortably furnished, the unpleasant odors I anticipated were absent, and the attendants were well-mannered and solicitous in their attention to me. I told them what I wanted, and a young woman then took me to the kitten room. It was bright and airy, with plenty of food and water bowls, toys and bedding material for the thirty or forty kittens present. Among them all, however, there was only one calico, off by herself for the moment, snoozing. I picked her up; she squirmed and meowed a bit, and I told the young woman that this was the kitten I wanted. I named her Samantha on the spot and began the walk back to the waiting room. On the way I asked the attendant what happened to so many kittens waiting for homes. She paused a moment, twitched her head, eyes wet, and said, "We keep each group about three weeks, sometimes longer, depending on the time of year. After that, we kill the ones we can't place with lethal injections. That's one of my jobs, and I hate it more than anything in the world. There's only so much space and funds available." When she had finished I held Samantha more closely to my chest.

Back in the waiting room I sat down while Samantha was taken for a physical examination, flea dusting, and initial inoculations. I began looking at some of the signs and posters on the wall, many of them meant to endear kittens and puppies to human hearts. But I came to one and stopped cold. It was a simple handwritten notice recording a simple heart-rending fact: from the beginning of that year until August 1 (the previous week) over five thousand animals had been killed (the author preferred, "put down") in just that one branch alone of the society. Beneath it was a further notice begging everyone to have their pets spayed or neutered to prevent the birth each year of millions of unwanted puppies and kittens. I stared at both signs for long moments, weary of still another reminder of human self-concern: let the dog or cat get pregnant so Junior will have a lesson in the processes of gestation, birth, and maternal care; sure, the babies are cute, but when they get older we can always drop them off at the Humane Society; it's best for them that way. These are baby animals allowed to be born only, so they can die six months later because of spoken but fraudulent human concern.

I cannot say I learned compassion for animals while sitting in that waiting room; it was, after all, only six years ago. But what did happen is that my compassion took on a sharper edge, a more robust and accusatory tone when addressing the refusal of even the slightest effort on the part of people to prevent so much death by taking steps to prevent too much life. It is the same compassion, I admit much stronger, that I have toward battered human children, the same accusation against their parents refusing responsibility they should never have taken on, without the claptrap of psychological excuse-making. Jesus says that not a sparrow falls to the ground without God knowing it, implying God's compassion toward the death of all creatures. Knowing the facts about the pointless death of baby animals, like knowing the facts about the mindless battering of baby humans, can issue in a shrug, a vocal but inactive concern, or compassion. But if it is compassion that comes forth, then only one choice is its twin: something must be done, however much it may be in each of our lives, to alter these facts. For knowing the facts, and doing nothing, is to gain the curse of accomplice.

A number of years ago I was driving to a store early one summer evening. In the car in front of me there was a group of four teenage boys. They were being raucous and playful with each other, the radio turned up to a deafening level, and each drinking from cans that I was sure did not contain soda or fruit juice. I kept my distance from them, as teenage drivers make me nervous, especially boys using the car as a sign of their freedom and machismo. Anyway, it wasn't far before I would reach the turnoff to the store, just after one more bend in the road. As I approached this bend my angle of view allowed me to see that up ahead, beyond the car in front of me, a small animal was walking on the road by the curb. As was my custom I intended to slow down at that point to shoo the animal off the street into safer terrain. For no matter how educable in other areas, most animals refuse to acknowledge the danger of moving automobiles, unless having survived a hit by one.

But to my complete horror the car in front of me suddenly veered sharply to the right. I heard the thumping sound when the animal was struck, for a second or two saw it bounce around under the car, then watched as it was spewed from the back of the car onto a nearby lawn. I came to a quick stop, and so did the car in front of me. For an instant I thought the driver might be feeling remorse for what he had done and wished to see if there was any help the animal, a raccoon as it turned out, might be given. Instead, the boy sitting next to the driver reached out and threw one of the cans that, with the damned perversity of luck, hit the raccoon square on the head. The boy then yelled, "Take that, you bastard!" and the car was gunned and screeched away. I got out and went over to the animal. She was dead, blood spilling from her mouth, and a little distance away, two of the babies she was carrying, dead also. The half-filled can of beer by her head was like a tombstone dedicated to the savagery of human behavior.

There are different types of anger. There is manipulative anger, that of the intellectual bully whose voice gets increasingly insistent, often accompanied by great rhetorical flourish, until you are cowed into submission to his or her viewpoint simply to have some quiet. All intellectual bullies know this effect. They are not really angry with you, but use the tones of anger, facial expressions too, because they desperately want your consent to their opinion and, with it, a sense of mastery over you. And then there is brooding anger, that of the individual who allows a hurt of years gone by to remain freshly painful because it is brooded over, tended to on a regular basis. This is the anger of two sisters I know who haven't spoken to each other for twenty years because of an argument they once had over a dress. And it has been bolstered by other putative affronts, the failure to send a Christmas card, to give notice of a baby's birth, to inform of a change of address. This is anger when it has become a way of life and requires what pastoral care calls a healing of memories. It is also an example of something noted in chapter one, when we suggested that Jesus saw triviality as one of the two fundamental sources of human evil, the other being discord.

But there is also righteous anger, justified anger before an intolerable offense that, were the offense greeted with tolerance or indifference, would make it all the worse. This is the anger I felt, and still feel, toward those teenage boys. In fact, there was a brief moment before they sped away when I felt blind anger, another type, and I thought that if I had a gun I would have shot the driver, not to kill but to cripple, in the kneecap or elbow, so he would have a permanent reminder of the evil he had done. It was righteous anger that caused Jesus to drive the buyers and sellers from the temple, the same that caused him to rebuke Peter for trying to deflect him from his destiny. I never saw those teenage boys again, so my anger, while justified, remained unproductive, merely festering in my spirit. There are situations we witness that we must shout against, in controlled fury and tempered outrage, when the persuasion of reasoned argument is inappropriate until a later time. Such was the case when drunken boys deliberately killed a mother raccoon for no other reason than the grotesque sport of it. I could only cry God's mercy on them, while still screaming a need for vengeance.

It is strange how disparate experiences can sometimes blend together, shaping a union among our values. It is not just strange, however, it is also wonderful, giving us a sense of wholeness in how we guide our lives, a wholeness we previously described as salvation. In our attitude toward animals this blending can occur when the compassion we want them shown is linked to righteous anger when this compassion is ignored or ridiculed. I have learned the truth of this more than once, in many various ways, but once I learned it from a room full of frisky kittens and a dead raccoon by the side of the road.

༄

I have been suggesting throughout these pages that the retrieval of memories is critical to any adequate assessment of what we have become. This is as true of individuals as it is of societies. It is the reason, for example, why the Jews celebrate a yearly Passover recollecting the events surrounding the exodus from Egypt, the time, they believe, when God clearly set them apart from all others as a chosen people with a promised land. Their memory strengthens them, accords them confidence in a world that more often than not has treated them with open hostility. It is the same reason Christians celebrate a Eucharist recollecting the events surrounding the life and death of Jesus, the privileged time, they believe, when God redeemed the world of sin by setting before us a path to salvation. Their memory, too, strengthens them, accords them confidence in a world that, while it has not treated them with the same hostility shown the Jews, regularly berates their belief of what was accomplished by the Nazarene.

Some would suggest that this retrieval of memories gives us our only proper definition of the meaning of resurrection from the dead. Anyone lives on after death only to the extent that others still living remember him or her, the sayings and deeds of a life now spent. And this is as true of Jesus or Buddha or Moses as it is of you and me, my pet cats, the rose you wore at your first dance. I have no argument with this suggestion, as far as it goes, since I think it captures the importance of memory, which I also have been emphasizing in these pages. It is just that I don't think it goes far enough. It confines resurrection to a completely anthropological dimension, whereas I would want to give it a theological dimension as well. In other words, resurrection is not only something we assure by our memories of what has passed, it is also something God assures by our faith in what will come to pass. Until God acts some few will stay alive in the memories of others; when God acts all that has lived will be alive again, not just in memory but in reality, living companions in a new existence. If this is not so, then with Dostoevsky I respectfully return the ticket, wishing no passage through time on God's train.

The memory I now have in mind is of an ant farm and three beehives I kept for a brief time while in high school. The insects fascinated me, the dexterity of their movements, the way they were able to live in such close quarters without seeming to get in each other's way, the configurations of their bodies, their protectiveness of their homes. But above all what fascinated me was their physical stamina, their diligence in carrying out their various tasks. As I said, I was in high school, and like nearly all teenagers I have known, diligence was not my strong suit. Perseverance was something associated with martyrs, a group of people who have always made me nervous. I preferred living each day as it came, getting through its basic demands with the least amount of effort, and daydreaming. This last especially occupied my time, fashioning destinies for myself that a kindly Fate would secure without asking my help. I was, to put it bluntly, lazy, prey to the indolence of adolescent youth dispirited by body changes and a growing awareness of the malfeasance of adults.

But the ants and bees bothered me. Their lives, I thought, were even worse off than mine, and yet they still labored, dumb, brute animals who nonetheless were showing greater interest in life than I was. Their behavior aggravated me, until it finally enlightened me. The enlightenment, however, came not first from them but from a simple mayfly that had managed one night to get into my bedroom. I watched its low, graceful flight for several moments, then went to bed, certain that the plants in the room would give it nourishment. When I awoke the following morning I found the mayfly dead on top of my desk. For some reason I became quite disturbed by the discovery, and while at school that day asked the biology teacher what might have happened to kill the insect. She said the cause was probably old age, as the life expectancy of mayflies was only a few days. I was dumbfounded more by the matter-of-factness than the cruelty of this truth that a creature could be born, suffer life's struggles for a few days, though once giving pleasure to a teenage lad watching its flight in his bedroom, then die. I knew that some lives were shorter than others, but this was the first time I learned just how short some of them were.

That little mayfly taught me a large lesson: no matter how long my life might last, it would not last long enough. And the ants and bees taught me as well that in the face of life's fleetingness we must apply ourselves diligently to the tasks we have set ourselves. These are old-fashioned truths, able to be learned from many sources, but they were learned by at least one teenage boy from insects who began awakening him from his adolescent slumbers. And when similar slumbers again entice the man the boy has become, the memory of ants and bees and mayflies keeps him awake, alert to his tasks, and thankful for the time spent and the time left in a world where beauty and life will one day prevail over their opponents. This is why I still keep that ticket I mentioned a short while ago.

For several years I used to spend a few weeks each summer at a camp in Maryland. It was a beautiful locale, woods full of trees, open meadows, and a spectacular lake bordering the property. I would take long walks over the land, as I have always found movement rather than stillness more conducive to productive meditation. A number of my previous books were born on those walks, and some of my most memorable experiences of animals. Composure is not something our culture values very highly, a centeredness of spirit overcoming the fragmentation, the splitting of our lives into many directions, that is frequently our lot. But on those forest and meadow walks I found composure, and now, years later, a certain bleak nostalgia bothers my mind for the few times, in different places, I have found the same. My life reads like a play whose acts, while understandable in themselves, are nonetheless incongruent with each other. I am not saying this is necessarily bad; I am only saying it disturbs me. It is as if my life has not yet been saved, made whole.

One summer somebody had set up a salt lick behind one of the buildings on the campground. It was meant to attract deer, and it did. I remember spending large parts of some afternoons shielded by a makeshift blind watching them. Their body forms were beautiful, their fur richly tawny, sometimes splashed with white on the chest and forehead. Their feet struck me as being rather small, even undersized for the body they had to carry, but the ears seemed disproportionately large. It was these ears that fascinated me the most. They were in constant movement, usually not synchronized with each other, always alert to any sound in the vicinity. If the sound was unfamiliar, the deer would stop licking at the salt, turn its head in the direction of the sound, with ears now working in tandem, pointing in the same direction as the head. In my makeshift blind, therefore, I had to remain not only unseen but unheard; otherwise my afternoon's delight could come to an abrupt end with the deer's flight.

I have noticed this same vigilance, of course, in other animals; in fact, in nearly all other animals. They are attuned to their environments in remarkably responsive ways, continually on watch for possible sources of food, wary of possible menace. Success in each depends on the extent of the animal's adeptness, for cautious deer are still taken by cats, wily rabbits still captured by hawks, and all animals prey to the cleverness and wit of human hunters. Vigilance is a way of life in the world of animals. What rest they can secure is for many a gamble that safety will remain, what playfulness engaged an opportunity for lurking threats. Old age, too, a time we like to hope for ourselves will be one of leisure and relaxation, holds no such hope for any other animal. Just the opposite is the case: if the animal is to stay alive longer, its vigilance must remain as acute as ever, not slacken. But this requires an effort, we know, that eventually always fails, and continued survival becomes mostly a matter of dumb luck.

I have spoken of the need for perseverance in the tasks we have set ourselves in an uncertain lifespan, drawing a lesson from ants and bees and mayflies. Now I would like to wed this perseverance to the vigilance I witnessed in a deer at a salt lick. One reason I do so is that if the old Greeks taught us that the unexamined life is not worth living (thus requiring vigilance), the old Hebrews taught us that the uncommitted life is not worth examining (thus requiring perseverance). We must seek to become as aware as we can of those things in our environment that can nourish us in our tasks, and those things that threaten us. It is my hope, of course, that all of us share as one of these tasks the care of animals, and that our perseverance and vigilance in carrying it out will become a song of praise and gratitude to the living presence of all God's creatures. There are those who would shout against such a song, trying to drown it out with indifference or contempt. We must then sing even louder, a psalmody whose music tells that the Earth is not ours alone but shared, with reverence due all life as reverence is due life's Maker. Care can sing no other song.

I have returned above to a theme, reverence for life, that has been with us since the beginning of this book. Reverence is like love; it is not something that falls from the sky free for our taking. It is something we must work at, a spiritual task needing perseverance and vigilance if it is to grow stronger and become expansive, embracing more and more of living things, ever more the living God. Any spirituality of animal care must make this reverence a part of the repertoire of its accomplishments, or at least of its pursuits, needing to nourish it — or just bring it alive — in everyone the spirituality touches. For the song of care is also a love song and a song of reverence, and in all the world of human beings it should have no audience but only participants, singing with one voice, comfort yet passion in their common task, the veneration of life.

CHAPTER EIGHT

❧

Sitting at Table as Equals

❧

We have travelled many places in this book, from wooded ponds to slaughterhouses to zoos and experimental laboratories. Everywhere we have gone we have met animals, all kinds of animals, and on the basis of the experiences they provided we have attempted to construct a spirituality of animal care. In doing so we have seen something of beauty, fidelity, and love, but also of horror, indifference, and contempt. But we have learned from our experiences only if we have allowed them a teaching role and ourselves a spirit of docility. Otherwise, like all our experiences, their lessons remain sterile or are forced upon us against our will. Some people are convinced the world has nothing more to teach them; for them this book is either useless or an unfriendly challenge. For others, though, the world is an endless source of wonder, and like the inquisitive children all of us once were, they question its ways and search out its mysteries. For them this book may have given insight, provoking assessment of old visions and values, leading the mind to firmer resolutions regarding attitudes toward animal care. An author cannot compel readers to a certain viewpoint; writing can only be an invitation to share and take seriously what the author offers.

In old mythologies the Earth, sea, and sky were especially worshipped as the milieus in which human life is nourished. And this makes sense; the three of them, after all, compose the primary ingredients making up the planet. I have looked to the inhabitants of each for lessons they might teach, land and water and sky dwellers, and have recorded some of them in this book. But there are many other lessons not spoken here. That is the way it is with writing; some selection is necessary, selecting in and out, because time and space are limited, and there are other interests to pursue. Every author of a book like this, therefore, must in one sense apologize to the readers, not so much for things committed as for things omitted. Perhaps in another time, other contexts, I will be able to share with you some of these other lessons I have come upon from my experiences with animals. But for now I think that what I have offered is sufficient to form the contours of a spirituality of animal care, which, were I asked, I could argue at greater length.

The sympathy for animals that this book encourages has a certain ineffability about it. It is the same ineffability we discover in our sympathetic relationships with other human beings. By this I mean that a point is eventually reached where one can no longer put into words an adequate description of the relationships. No matter how eloquent and detailed one has been, to the question, "Is that all there is; have you fully described the relationship?" the response remains, "No, there is more, but I just can't put it into words." It is this ineffability that Gabriel Marcel calls a mystery, what is known or felt but cannot be fully diagnosed in satisfying ways. Something is always missing and what is missing is the mystery, and the mystery is ourselves. To ask for a complete description of a relationship we have is to ask for a complete description of ourselves in the relationship. And this is something that escapes us, a task we cannot fulfill.

So for generations mystics have tried to capture in words their union with God, and have always come up short. Others have tried to do so regarding their union with another human being — Shakespeare, for example, with the lady of his sonnets — with a similar result. Musicians and painters, too, confess inadequacy when attempting to articulate their relationship to their art. And I must confess the same about what animals mean to me. Such confessions, however, indicate not only the personal involvement of the individual in the relationship, but the very richness of experience that the other in the relationship offers, whether it be God, music, sculpted stone, painted canvas, or owls with broken wings. We know the relationship exists, we know its effects on us and the interests it creates, but we do not know how to share these fully with someone else. This can lead to frustration, even anger, especially in human relationships, but eventually it leads to the awareness that our inability is a simple fact we must accept. If not, the frustration will only fester, the anger will turn to brooding, and both will become a waste of time.

We must, then, face the limits of what we can do; and this is true of all our activities, not just the attempts to express the meaning of our relationships. But these limits, while always present to some degree, can nonetheless be expanded to the extent that we bring others into our activities, just as our ability to describe relationships is expanded by engaging thoughts other than our own, in study or conversation. Yet if we are to attract others to points of view and their attendant actions that we deem worthy, we must seek to become as persuasive as we can, in both word and deed, when representing ourselves. It is a major hope of this book that I have exercised such persuasion — if not in deeds here, at least in words — with regard to the structuring of an effective spirituality of animal care. For if I can attract others into this spirituality, then my limits in working out its repercussions can be overcome by the efforts of others doing the same. In other words, like every other productive spirituality, this one too must be both individually and communally oriented.

A spirituality need not be attached to religion, as a number of illustrations would show: Confucianism and some forms of Buddhism, Camus's existentialism of rebellion and Sartre's of atheistic humanism, Marxism untouched by Lenin, Stalin, or Mao. In this book, however, I have chosen to link the spirituality in a number of places with assertions about God drawn principally from Judeo-Christian tradition. I have done so because I believe this type of linkage provides us with a richer resource for understanding ourselves and our world than we would have in its absence. And I have chosen the Judeo-Christian tradition simply because it is the one with which I am most familiar, though here and there I have also felt free to draw on insights from Buddhism. On the other hand, I think the book is written so that it can enliven those of other religious traditions — or those who follow none at all, but who nonetheless have an interest in animal care.

But having said this, I must now say that Christianity in particular — at least in its sources and major theological traditions — has very little to offer a spirituality of animal care in a direct, unambiguous fashion; in fact, many of the teachings are either indifferent to or openly contemptuous of such a spirituality. True, we can say some things with considerable certainty about Jesus' own attitude toward animals. He does find it useful now and then to employ them in his parables and exhortations, but not always in positive ways, to illustrate the point he is making or the judgment he is offering. True also is the fact that he did not participate in animal sacrifice in the temple; he seemed openly scornful of it and insisted that his disciples follow his example. But it is likely that his purpose here was more to redress the barbarous image of God these sacrifices implied than to spare animals from the knife and altar.

It is indeed in the image of God they promote that I suspect Jesus' teachings have the most value for a spirituality of animal care. This God is passive, that is, receptive and responsive to events in the world, motivated in behavior by a love that has precedence even over justice. And this love is not confined to, though it is principally concerned with, the human inhabitants of the world. Instead, it extends its embrace over all living things, imbuing them with varying degrees of freedom and beauty, trying to persuade all toward goodness. In previous chapters we have seen some of the results of this theological stance, its implications for our treatment of animals, as well as each other, and the obligations it therefore places on us. It is a costly and difficult love this God of Jesus both demonstrates and encourages, not the cheap and easy love of dimestore novels and romantic philosophies. I suppose this is why it appeals to some but is unendurable by others.

There seeped very early into Christianity the influence of Greek thought, especially its forms of metaphysics; the seepage soon became a flood. One of the areas where this influence exercised its greatest power was in the Christian doctrine of God, so that the passive, receptive God of Jesus (and of all Judaism) was soon transmuted into the impassive, unreceptive God of classical theism. This is a God who is indifferent to happenings in the world, uncaring about such things as how we brutalize and slaughter animals, or even ourselves — because caring about them is seen as a type of contamination of God's glory, a sullying of God's being by too close an association with the created yet imperfect world. The invasion of this viewpoint into Christian theologies that also wished to remain true to the witness of Jesus produced not just illogic in presentations of Christian belief but a spiritual schizophrenia in Christian minds. God is to be thought of as impassive, uninfluenced by what we do, yet we are still encouraged to offer prayers of petition. And despite the subtle mental gymnastics of many to harmonize the two viewpoints, their efforts amount to little more than theological trickery. We cannot have it both ways with God, which for Christians means we must choose the way of Jesus.

It is to the distinction of Thomas Aquinas that he is the one often hailed as succeeding in the proper use of Greek metaphysics, especially that of Aristotle, to produce a Christian doctrine of God that does not contradict the teachings of Jesus. I am not certain about this, nor are many others. What I am certain about is that Aquinas argued a hierarchy of souls in creation (vegetative, animal, and rational souls) and that only rational souls, those in human beings, had true worth in the eyes of God — so that only they, for example, reunited with their bodies, would be raised from the dead. And I am also certain that the enormous influence he had in ensuing centuries (not just he, of course, but others too, before and afterward) contributed to the devaluing of animal life until animals became little more than the playthings of human whim, and little or no morality was attached to how they were treated, save in a few rare cases. Aquinas may be extolled by some as the Angelic Doctor in Christian history, but for those concerned with a spirituality of animal care his reputation, and that of his sympathizers, is far more dubious.

While it is true, then, that there are some instances in Christian tradition where due reverence has been given to animals, for the most part this is not so. If this situation is to be corrected, one of the things needed is to abandon parts of the Greek metaphysics upon which so much of Christian thought is still being built, especially the metaphysics of an impassive God and the typology of souls or spirits. This is what Leslie Dewart once called the task of "de-hellenizing" Christian philosophy and theology. To the old Greeks we owe much for their gifts to how we think, perhaps nowhere more than in their abiding conviction that the unexamined life is not worth living. But as I said in the last chapter, to this conviction we must add at once the biblical judgment that the uncommitted life is not worth examining. So this book has been an attempt both to examine how it is we treat animals and to encourage commitment to their proper care. If at points, therefore, it has made you laugh or weep, made you satisfied or angry, and in the process has encouraged your attentiveness and commitment to a spirituality of animal care, it has been a success.

I once knew a very old priest who was worn out by life. He had been on battlefields of human warfare, had counselled many to peace of mind, cultured an exquisite talent for the violin, written fine contributions to his field of scholarship, and he had prayed more in his one life than I would in five of mine. His back was bent, hands and legs arthritic, white hair thinned, a chronic melancholy pooling in his eyes, living proof of the meanness of old age. One day he said to me he could not remember ever intentionally damaging another living thing, human or non-human. It was not a boast; he was too old and too wise to boast about himself. It was the confession of a simple fact, and it seemed to lend him contentment about how he had conducted his life — a contentment he displayed at no other time when discussing himself. I used to look forward to my time with him, drinking delicious teas or a touch of brandy, listening to his accounts of a rich and gentle existence. He was the person second closest to saintliness I have ever known.

The old priest had a canary, a companion of eleven years whose cage door was always left open, giving free access to the rooms of the apartment. The canary preferred to be on the floor, scurrying around for dropped tidbits of food or just to examine objects he had already examined countless times. One day while reading a book in his rocking chair the old priest tilted back and crushed the canary under one of the rockers of the chair. Two days later when I visited him he would only talk about what his brother had meant to him and how he had carelessly killed him. This use of the word "brother" reminded me of the kinship Francis of Assisi felt for animals, his prayers celebrating this kinship, and his desire that it be shared by everyone. Three days after I visited him, the old priest had a stroke, and the day after he died. Those with him during the three days he was still conscious confirmed that to the last he spoke only of his sorrow for the death of his companion. Nothing anyone said consoled him; his final thoughts were of grief and guilt, the ending of a beautiful life sad beyond words.

What the old priest taught me in a crystalline way was that a feeling of kinship is the key to unlocking the meaning of any spirituality of animal care, a kinship born of gratitude and compassion, a sense of beauty and loving kindness, mutual need and shared place — all the many components of kinship I have done my best to honor and describe in this book. Family is the concept I have sought to control my analysis, the whole Earth composed of kindred beings, the stronger aiding the weak, the brighter assisting the less adept, those who love reaching out to those who cannot, self-sacrifice valued more highly than self-interest. It is not just family, then, that I have sought out in these reflections, but a good family, which, when God is believed its begetter, becomes a holy family.

I close now with a quotation from Kierkegaard, whose books I cherish, and a thought of my own. Kierkegaard writes, "It is a far less dreadful thing to fall on your knees when the mountains tremble with the voice of God than to sit at table with him as an equal; and yet it is precisely God's will to have it so." If the dreadfulness of sitting down with God as an equal, the awesomeness of the act wherein the difference between deity and humanity is bridged, occurs because of God's loving will, a similar human will can bridge the lesser difference between ourselves and the animals who are our kindred in the broad compass of life. My closing thought, then, is precisely this, our willingness to have it so.